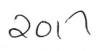

DATE DUE

2017

Praise for *Not Safe for Church*

"Douglas Powe and Jasmine Smothers are voices of 'NOW,' and *Not Safe for Church* is an urgent book for NOW. They are two people I respect immensely and their collective experience offers new insight to old traditions. It's been said 80 percent of funds supporting church ministry today comes from people over fifty-five years of age. It's safe to say this signals the fact the church has entered a perilous era of irrelevance to a broad spectrum of young people in America and beyond. This book is not only challenging but also compelling and timely. You will no doubt be moved to see the church like you have never seen the church before."

—**Rudy Rasmus**, Senior Pastor,
St. John's United Methodist Church, Houston, TX

"Reaching out to new generations is fundamental if the church is really seeking to make disciples of Jesus Christ for the transformation of the world. We can be grateful to Doug Powe and Jasmine Smothers for calling Christians to follow Christ's great commandment by boldly engaging in ten challenging covenant practices that are worth taking a risk to engage. Read, risk, and reach out in Jesus's name!"

—**Bishop B. Michael Watson**, North Georgia Episcopal Area,
United Methodist Church

"The church is always looking for fresh perspectives on how to bridge the chasm that exists between the generations within the church and society. Jasmine and Doug share a provocative theological framework and provide practical ways to engage in meaningful ministry with the post-civil rights generations. They boldly and prophetically challenge the church to confront the status quo. This book is a must-read for pastors, church leaders, and seminarians."

—**Tracy S. Malone**, District Superintendent of the Chicago Southern District,
Northern Illinois Conference, United Methodist Church

"*Not Safe for Church* is a dynamic and straightforward resource for any congregation seeking to facilitate constructive changes toward the millennial generation in the African American church. Powe and Smothers offer ten distinct and actionable strategies that congregations can wrestle with in order for churches to engage younger adults. While tailored to the African American church, any church would be wise to give careful attention to each of the commandments in its approach for relevance in the twenty-first century. The book's list of commandments is carefully crafted and accessible for church leaders and educators who are seeking ways to dialogue about change and engagement of young adults. I look forward to engaging these commandments in both the classroom and the parish."

—**Asa J. Lee**, Assistant Director for Programs, Lewis Center for Church
Leadership, Wesley Theological Seminary, Washington, DC

F. Douglas Powe Jr.
& Jasmine Rose Smothers

209598

Ten Commandments for
Reaching New Generations

Abingdon Press
Nashville

NOT SAFE FOR CHURCH:
TEN COMMANDMENTS FOR REACHING NEW GENERATIONS

This book is printed on acid-free paper.

Library of Congress Cataloging-in-Publication Data

Powe, F. Douglas.
    Not safe for church : ten commandments for reaching new generations / F. Douglas Powe Jr. and Jasmine Rose Smothers.
       pages cm
    ISBN 978-1-4267-7576-5 (binding: soft back, trade pbk. : alk. paper)
    1. Church renewal.   2. Intergenerational relations—Religious aspects—Christianity.   3. Church work with young adults.   I. Title.
    BV600.3.P69 2015
    259'.2—dc23
                                                                            2014031626

15 16 17 18 19 20 21 22 23 24—10 9 8 7 6 5 4 3 2 1
MANUFACTURED IN THE UNITED STATES OF AMERICA

I (Doug) dedicate this book to Rev. Rodney Smothers, who has been a great mentor in ministry.

I (Jasmine) dedicate this book to Dr. Jacqueline Rose-Tucker (Mom) and Dr. Rodney Smothers (Dad) who were my first pastors, teachers, coaches, and models for excellence in serving God, the beloved people of God, and the church. And to my brother and sister, for whom I dream of a more authentic and life-giving church.

Contents

Introduction

Many of us have been sitting at our computers at work when all of a sudden a message flashes from a friend and in the title it says—**NSFW!** Not Safe for Work! Typically this means one of our friends thinks something is worth viewing, but it is probably better viewed in a safe space outside of work. To be blunt, opening the message is a risk that could get you in trouble with your employer. How many of us take the risk and open the message? Maybe we have smartphones and view it on the phones and not on our work computers. The truth is, for many of us the curiosity is just too much; we need to know what is in the message.

This book is sending a message to congregations and the subject title reads—**NSFC!** *Not Safe for Church!* If you continue reading, then you should do so at your own risk. You may get in trouble if you keep going, because it is going to make you think and act differently. The best way to proceed may be to keep this book or your e-reader hidden so others do not see you viewing such material. Of course, you can do like many at work who receive such messages: be bold and share it with others. Let's be honest, there is something special about being a risk taker in the right way.

In the book of Numbers we find Caleb and Joshua who are the right kind of risk takers. In Numbers 13, Moses sends twelve spies (one from each tribe of Israel) to determine if the land in Canaan is worth inhabiting. We realize the implications of taking the land of other nations and are not downplaying this fact, but hope readers can focus on the way in which the reports are given. All of the spies agree that the land is bountiful; verse 27 says, "it flows with milk and honey." The difference is most of the spies are afraid and perceive Canaan as unsafe; it is safer not to enter Canaan. Caleb gives the minority report and says the Israelites should go at once to occupy the land. Caleb knows there is a risk, but perceives the risk to be good (or worth it) because God has already promised the Israelites the land.

For Caleb and Joshua, the real danger or adverse action lies in not following God. The other spies perceived the risk as too great because in their minds they can maintain the status quo without any consequences. We learn in Deuteronomy 1:19-36 that Caleb was right and the spies, who thought maintaining the status quo was safe, were wrong. With the exception of Joshua, the other spies were afraid to act because not acting seemed the safer choice. It is not that they could not understand the possibilities of entering into Canaan, rather it was their fear of losing what they had. Many of our congregations are like the majority report of the spies who are afraid to act. They know things need to change, but actually doing something seems unsafe.

Thinking and acting in new ways is not safe for many congregations. We do not simply mean moving away from a 1950s mentality—more and more congregations are grasping that things have indeed changed since sixty years ago. What we do mean is to issue an invitational challenge to congregations, so that they think and act differently when it comes to reaching post-civil rights generations (those born after 1961). The fruit of this shift is a willingness to take risks and to open our minds to new ideas that will cause us to do things differently. To be like Caleb and Joshua, not only seeing the possibilities, but being willing to act on the possibilities. For congregations this means redefining the ways in which we understand worship, spiritual growth opportunities, and becoming followers of Jesus.

It is safe to redefine worship in terms of traditional versus something more contemporary. What is not safe is suggesting that it is time to move beyond two options. It is safe to redefine spiritual growth opportunities as post-civil rights generations plugging into existing classes or having their own classes. What is not safe is suggesting that the way we approach the curriculum or spiritual growth opportunities has to change. It is safe to redefine being a follower of Jesus as someone who makes contributions to the life of the congregation. What is not safe is suggesting the congregation make a contribution to those who will not darken the doors of the church.

We repeat, this book is NSFC! It is going to persuade you to think and act differently in order to connect with the post-civil rights generations. We recognize there are a few challenges or hiccups that some of you will need to address up front. If you do not want to simply fall prey to the majority report like the Israelites, then you will have to confront these challenges. **There are some congregations that are afraid of connecting with the post-civil rights generations, because they literally believe that those generations are not safe for the church.** Some in the post-civil rights generations do not look like us. They wear different clothing, have various piercings, and are tatted up.[1] They are not safe for our congregations.

If we are judging who is acceptable by their appearances, then Peter, Andrew, James, and John may have been excluded from many of our congregations. In Matthew 4:18-22, it talks about Jesus calling the two sets of brothers down by the Sea of Galilee. They were fishermen, meaning they probably did not look, smell, or talk like the "good temple" people of the day. We cannot get stuck on appearances for determining who is safe or not safe for church. Jesus could have called anyone to be his first disciples, but Jesus calls those whom many would have perceived as unsafe.

There are other congregations seeking to play it safe because they fear too many new ideas will make church unfamiliar for them. This sentiment often gets expressed by the phrase, "What about me?" Those inside the church are worried that they have been forgotten and everything is geared toward new folk. Those inside the church want to remind the powers that be that they have been faithful for years and should not be discounted at this point.

Jesus helps us frame this "What about me?" sentiment differently. In Matthew 5:16-20, Jesus states he has not come to abolish the law but to fulfill it. The concern by some is that Jesus is moving ahead too quickly and changing everything familiar to them. Jesus's statement in Matthew 5:16-20 follows the Beatitudes (Matt 5:3-12), where Jesus turns upside down those who are truly blessed. Jesus reminds us that everything being proposed is in line with and meant to fulfill the Law.

Jesus does not apologize for making some uncomfortable who wanted things to stay exactly the same, but he does bring comfort and give us the grace to practice the essentials of our faith. For those who want a safe church where everything is the same, this book will make you uncomfortable. For those who are seeking familiarity in terms of maintaining some of their traditions, this book will help you generate new ideas for connecting with the post-civil rights generations. In following Jesus, we believe there is a difference between familiarity and just doing things the ways we've always done them. Those who want to play it safe want to do the exact same thing and are happy to accept the fact that nothing will change.

A major reason many congregations play it safe is the famous phrase, "We tried it once, and it did not work." Many congregations get excited and attempt something new. They move forward, but the project goes nowhere. It fails miserably! No one new shows up or only a couple of new people show up. The next time a similar idea is proposed, the congregation prefers to play it safe and not attempt anything, because "we already tried." Of course, when they experience this repeatedly, a congregation can get stuck in deep mud from which it cannot escape.

The rich young ruler (Matt 19:16-26) had a similar experience when encountering Jesus. The rich young ruler wanted to inherit eternal life and asked Jesus what he needed to do. Jesus tells him to follow the commandments, which the ruler replied he already does. Jesus tells him to sell all his possessions and to follow him. But upon hearing these words, the ruler goes away sad. The ruler could not let go of his possessions; he wanted to follow Jesus, but he was stuck in a place where he could not move forward. Following Jesus was exciting, but letting go of what he had was too huge a risk—he was stuck in the mud unable to move forward. Many congregations are stuck in this same place because they want to play it safe and not try new things. These congregations are content to simply say, "We tried that" or "We already do that" and use their past as an excuse not to move forward.

Given these challenges, how can congregations move forward? Interestingly enough, in Deuteronomy 1:19 and following, the story of the twelve spies is summarized by Moses. He uses this story as a reminder for the Israelites to stay obedient to God. Then in chapter five, Moses repeats the Ten Commandments. The Ten Commandments helped structure the lives and community of the Israelites. Moses tells the Israelites that the way forward is by adhering to the Ten Commandments by trusting God.

We are not Moses, but we do believe the way forward for many congregations is paying attention to the ten commandments in this book. These commandments are covenant practices that will make you think and act differently.[2] These are practices that congregations can engage in together that will move them forward in a positive manner. We warn you again that following these commandments are NSFC and we dare you to try them.

First Commandment

Thou Shall Chill: What's at Stake

Chill: cool, tight, wicked, sweet, nice, etc., to hang out[1]

Have you ever been a part of a conversation or gathering where individuals seemed to be headed in very different directions? One group of people is busy planning and strategizing about what needs to take place. Another group is laid-back and seems disconnected from the conversation. Those in the first group get frustrated with those who are seemingly disconnected because they just do not seem to care. This is how some older generations experience the post-civil rights generations, as disconnected and laid-back. It often frustrates older generations!

The frustration in part is that those in the post-civil rights generations do not seem to understand what is at stake. In the Numbers 13 text, the other spies are frustrated with Caleb because he does not seem to grasp what is at stake in giving a positive report about the land (Num 13:30). The other spies understand the

1

"real" danger that Caleb does not. They do not understand why Caleb seems so nonchalant about the whole ordeal.

The issue is, "What really is at stake?" Do those in the post-civil rights generations really not get it? Or is it possible, many in the church misunderstand *chillin'?* We are suggesting, the challenge for many is how they understand chillin'. The negative side of chillin', for some, is a form of laziness. The positive side of chillin', for some, is a form of not taking one's self so seriously. The pendulum swinging between these two poles can cause tension and at times intense frustration by those locked into one side or the other. In this chapter, we explore the pendulum swinging back and forth and its implications for congregations.

What Is at Stake?

Many of us are familiar with the saying, "It takes two to fight!" The point being that it is hard to fight against yourself. Imagine two sides supposedly engaged in a tug-of-war and one side is entrenched, holding the rope tightly. The other side is relaxed and barely holding the rope. When the signal is given to start pulling, the side that is entrenched makes a huge pull and gets no resistance from the other side. Although the one side wins the tug-of-war, it is not a satisfying victory because the other team did not fight back.

Many churches feel like they are in a tug-of-war with the post-civil rights generations and unchurched individuals. Those in the church are entrenched and ready for battle, but their opponents are not engaged in the struggle. In part, this is because the struggle is about saving the church, which is not a fight many outside of the church are interested in participating in. What is at stake for those inside congregations is very different from those on the other end of the rope. It is only when congregations understand they are fighting against themselves that they can stop and rethink their actions. The New Testament story about the rich man helps congregations look in a mirror and let go of their entrenched position. It helps them chill!

In Mark 10:17-27, we find a story about a rich man (some translations say young man) who seeks eternal life. This man asks Jesus what is needed to achieve eternal life. Jesus responds by naming the Commandments and telling the rich man to hold fast to them. The rich man replies, "All these I have kept since I was a boy." This is where the story gets interesting: Jesus, in verse 21, says, "One thing you lack.... Go sell everything you have and give to the poor, and you will have treasure in heaven, Then come follow me." In verse 22, we are told the rich man is shocked by Jesus's words and leaves grieving.

The rich man initially goes to Jesus because he seeks salvation. Many of our congregations today are busy trying to save themselves. The challenge is they are trying to save themselves by staying in their comfort zone and never moving out. The rich man is seeking salvation, but doing so in a way that allows him to stay in his comfort zone. The idea of letting go of all of his possessions is too high a price to pay to follow Jesus. For the church, the idea of letting go of those things preventing us from following Jesus seems like a high price to pay.

I can imagine if Jesus had responded to continue to hold to the Commandments and give an offering to the poor, the rich man would have gladly done so. The fact that Jesus requires him to sell all of his possessions hits him like a ton of bricks. Many congregations are being asked to completely give up what they have known and follow Jesus. It is a high price. What is at stake is saving the congregation, but to give up everything seems unfair. Jesus is clear that this is the price, and the consequences for not paying are probably the eventual death of the congregation. The very thing that the congregation is trying to avoid may still become a reality because of an unwillingness to let go.

In Mark 10:23, Jesus confirms the challenge of letting go when he says how hard it is for a wealthy person to enter the kingdom of God. Jesus could have as easily stated, "How hard it is for a congregation to let go of old ways and to follow me toward a new future." The challenge for congregations is letting go of the very thing that seems at stake for them—saving the church. It is only when congregations are willing to let go that new possibilities can occur.

What does this mean practically for a congregation? How can entrenched congregations let go? Imagine a congregation that has a worship team of seasoned members planning a new "contemporary" worship. The team knows it needs to do something new because they are losing individuals to the congregation down the street doing a contemporary worship experience. They are excited and start planning for the grand launch!

As the launch draws closer, the worship team is frustrated because those in the post-civil rights generations or newer members seem disconnected and not as excited. They do not seem interested in the new service. The seasoned members cannot figure out why. The seasoned members are trying to give the people what is needed and they do not seem to want it.

Notice the seasoned members never ask any questions or have a dialogue with those in the post-civil rights generations or newer members. They decide what it is the congregation needs to do and set off on their own path. The reality is the seasoned members are not able to let go of being in charge and making all of the decisions. They are not able to "chill" and to create space for some new voices or ideas to take shape in the community. The underlying issue is they are so concerned about saving the congregation it is hard for them to let go and chill.

For many entrenched in saving a congregation chillin' seems counterintuitive. It makes no sense to take a step back and to let go. Those truly seeking to save their congregation are focused on taking action and going down fighting, even if no one is fighting against them on the other side of the rope. The ability to chill does not mean inaction, instead it is not overreacting to the current situation. If what is really at stake is saving the church, then learning to chill can be a congregation's best asset.

In the story of the rich man he went away grieving because he wanted eternal life on his terms. In a similar fashion, we want to save the congregation on our terms. We need to chill on doing things on our terms and have faith in Christ. Letting go and following Jesus is risky (not safe for many churches), but can lead to eternal life on God's terms. A congregation willing to let go and chill may be able to save the church, but it will not be on its own terms. The saving will be on God's terms. The question then is, "How do we let go?"

5

A New Spirit

Numbers 14:24 reads, "But because my servant Caleb has a different spirit and follows me wholeheartedly, I will bring him into the land he went to, and his descendants will inherit it." We are struck by the phrase *a different spirit.* One way of thinking about this phrase is that Caleb is completely in sync with God and others are not. Without denying that interpretation, we are suggesting that Caleb has a different understanding of what is at stake. Caleb believes a new future with God is at stake, while the other spies believe their mortal lives are at stake. Interestingly, both sets of spies are right, but in different ways.

The spies who bring the negative report are concerned about being defeated by the giants of the land and losing their lives (Num 13:32). What is at stake for them is their very existence. These spies are able to convince the other Israelites that they also should be concerned about their lives. A spirit of fear permeates most of the Israelites that leads to them staying in their comfort zone.

Caleb has a different spirit. Caleb believes in a new future with God so he sees things differently. When God forgives Israel for not believing, God mentions Caleb's different spirit in Numbers 14:24. We believe many in the post-civil rights generations like Caleb have a different spirit. In this particular instance, we are describing this spirit as one of chillin'. Many in the post-civil rights generations are not worried about the existence of the church as a matter of life or death. Many in these generations do believe in a new future with God.

It is hard for those currently in congregations to hear that many individuals coming from younger generations do not have the same life-or-death worry they do. Those in congregations, particularly those who have been a part of them for a while, want individuals to have the same love of the church that they do. For many who feel the younger generations do not have this love, it is perceived as a lack of commitment by those in the post-civil rights generations. Many in the church do not stop to consider that the post-civil rights generations do, in fact, have commitment, but it is not to a building. They, like Caleb, have a different spirit that is committed to seeking where God is leading.

Many in the post-civil rights generations or outside of the church believe life is not defined by the church building. Life is defined by following where it is that God is leading even if that means having no building. There is no question that once you have something and get used to it, it is hard to let go. Yet, when we idolize a building or something else material, we have missed the point of discipleship. Discipleship is about having the kind of spirit where we will follow Christ into the world and, most importantly, into our community. Discipleship is not about creating a comfort zone where we maintain the status quo. The question is, "Can we be re-formed to have a new spirit of chillin'?"

Re-Formation

The popularity of extreme sports continues to grow nationally. Skateboarding is one of the events that helped to make extreme sports popular. What is fascinating is the difference between a more traditional sport like football and skateboarding. Typically, if one watches even a sixth-grade football practice, the intensity in terms of players working hard and giving their all is noticeable. Compare this to a group of sixth graders hanging out, riding their skateboards, and working on different maneuvers; the intensity is very different. The skateboarders seem a lot more relaxed and not so high strung. Because they are laid-back, however, should not be taken as not taking their sport seriously.

If both groups take their sports seriously, then why would some individuals perceive football differently? One of the differences (in most instances) is skateboarders do not have coaches standing over them constantly giving and, at times, barking instructions. In football, it is clear who is in charge and the coach's intensity often is reflected in the structure and tone of practice. Typically, there is no set coach in skateboarding, so individuals are free to do their own thing or collaborate with others. Yet, the ultimate goal for a sixth grader in both sports is to make it to the highest level, which is the NFL or to qualify for extreme sports championships. The path to accomplishing this goal is often different because the way in which they are formed in the sport is typically different.

Someone watching the sixth-grade football practice versus sixth graders skateboarding may notice how the cultures are different. For a football player, participation at practice is mandatory as is following instructions and giving 110 percent. Generally speaking, at skateboarding practice one may notice collaborative instructions; you pick and choose your time; participation is voluntary. The way individuals are formed in the various cultures differs and this impacts attitudes and perceptions. For example, in football it is not acceptable for a healthy player to relax while teammates run wind sprints. If a player is healthy, then the expectation is the player will be out with the rest of the team giving all they have. In skateboarding, it is acceptable to watch as others do maneuvers and ride, without feeling guilty about not participating. In fact, one may pick up some things that are helpful when they start participating again.

Someone who is ingrained in the football culture and stops to watch skateboarding could easily draw some false conclusions. The fact that no one seems to be in charge can be perceived as not a serious practice. The fact that skateboarders, many times, don't seem to put a lot of effort into a run can be perceived as not giving 100 percent. The fact that a person may sit out for a while can be perceived as not fully participating or lazy. These are all conclusions that someone ingrained in a football culture could make, but they are not necessarily true.

The person ingrained in football culture is not purposely trying to demean the skateboarders but because of his or her formation in football, perceives things in a certain way. The person was formed in a culture where following directions, going all out, and full participation is important. But because of being formed in this way, it's more challenging to understand other ways of being formed. The truth is, other ways of being formed may not even make sense.

It's no wonder that in the church we struggle to understand those who are formed differently than we have been. Like those ingrained in football culture, we tend to see things from our church culture perspective. When someone seems disconnected and not going with the flow, instead of considering that this person may have been formed differently, we often just think negative thoughts about the person. The church starts making assumptions like those ingrained in football culture about how one should engage, and if an individual does not engage in the right way, then something is wrong with them.

The fact that individuals not a part of church culture may have been formed or shaped in a different way often does not cross our minds. We assume those outside of the church are going to be just like us. They will listen to given instructions, go all out, and, ideally, want to fully participate. The idea that these individuals may want to collaborate, test things out, and see where they fit in first may not cross our minds, so we call them names like *lazy* or *aloof*. If we associate terms like lazy and aloof with chillin', then chillin' can seem like a negative.

Before those of us in the church decide that chillin' is a bad thing, we should consider the importance of formation. Just because one does not demonstrate a particular intensity or fit a particular mold, we should not pigeonhole that person. It is possible to be chill and still seek to move forward toward a goal. The pendulum is not stuck on the negative side of chillin'. Certainly we are not suggesting all forms of chillin' are positive, but we are suggesting that one should not predetermine or prejudge that chillin' is bad.

Many in the church can learn from those formed to appreciate chillin' (the opposite is also true). By chillin' we can develop a different perspective on something instead of simply charging ahead. For many ingrained in a church culture, this means being reformed to work collaboratively and sometimes taking a step back to get a fuller sense of the picture. Doing these things may feel uncomfortable but could be life-giving to the congregation. For many in the church, it is a chance to meet on the bridge and start participating with those who are often silenced.

The First Commandment: Thou Shall Chill

The first commandment for reaching new generations is Thou Shall Chill. It is important for congregations to understand chillin', because in seeking to save the church we may be doing more damage. Developing a spirit of chillin' will enable many of us to be formed in different ways that will help us to become better disciples. Discipleship is not about staying in our comfort zones and protecting a building. Discipleship in this instance is about believing in a new future with God that requires us to chill and to let go of some things. In the following chapters, we will discuss those things that need to be let go. If we are so entrenched in holding on to certain things, then we cannot open our hearts to receiving new things. Thou Shall Chill on staying entrenched! We shall open our hearts to a new future with God.

Covenant Practice: Let Go

1. What are three ways in which your congregation is entrenched and not willing to let go?

2. Read Numbers 14:20-25. Who do you know who has a different spirit like Caleb? What are some of the traits that differentiate them from others?

3. How is your congregation collaborative and not so collaborative with the post-civil rights generations?

4. What would it look like if people in your congregation chilled?

5. What would be easy to let go of? What would be hard? What would be impossible?

Second Commandment

Thou Shall Not Front: Be Authentic

Front: To put on a fake or false personality; not keeping it real[1]

May I have your attention please?

Will the real Slim Shady please stand up, please stand up, please stand up?

> —*"The Real Slim Shady" by Eminem, Dr. Dre, and Tommy Coster*

In 2000, hip-hop artist Eminem topped the charts with his hit song, "The Real Slim Shady." The song was a response to a perceived trend of "fake" pop songs that were being produced at the time. The song demanded that the real, true, authentic artists in the music industry stand up and produce music that was real, true, and authentic. Just as the authors of this song challenged the music industry to take inventory of its authenticity and its motives, many of our churches today could stand to ask the hard question, "Will the real disciples please stand up?" Yet, congregations must do more than ask; they must require an answer.

In the Numbers 13 text, the spies in the wilderness had to answer a similar question. Were they true believers or simply *frontin'*? Joshua and Caleb were authentic to God's covenant with the Israelites. The other spies were frontin'. Too many congregations and individuals are frontin'. They are not authentic to God's mission and calling.

Unfortunately, this means many of our churches have lost their identity. Congregations have bowed to the pressures of consumer society and, in the name of survival, are working overtime to be all things to all people. As people are offered varying demands on their time, congregations are grappling with how to compete with the daily demands of work, family, school, soccer, band, basketball, and more. Congregations are forced to ask, how do we offer programming that is more interesting to our communities so that they will come? Church leaders are grappling with questions like: Are we entertainers? Are we parents? Are we equippers? How much can we expect from congregants and potential congregants? Can we expect members to be disciples? During this process, church leaders and parishioners have unintentionally thrust the church into an identity crisis. We have invested in the religious version of "get-rich-quick" schemes. We pull a little of what worked for this megachurch and that megachurch instead of investing our time in discerning what God is calling us to do in our own situation, in our own context, in our own time, with our own gifts, with our own hands, for such a time as this. Cherry-picking church growth strategies have left congregations on loose, misunderstood, or wavering theological grounding. Congregants no longer know what they believe and pick churches based on what looks good and is convenient or popular. In an effort to stay vital and pay the bills, it appears that churches have lost sight of the fact that God has gifted every congregation in different ways in order to serve in their context authentically.

Congregational Identity and Spiritual Propaganda

Some congregations have fallen prey to spiritual propaganda. Church politics and congregational competition have allowed congregations to forsake Christian mission and identity for corporate strategies and shiny programming. If it looks good to onlookers, draws the people, and makes our numbers balance, we'll choose that way without regard for mission or meaning. Unfortunately, in many places, we have listened to well-meaning leaders who have not always been faithful to the mission or have lost sight of the mission of making disciples. We have allowed the size of our church or the number of degrees in our pews to determine what kind of ministry we will engage in and with whom we will engage in that ministry. At the same time, the post-civil rights generations are begging the church to have an authentic voice and an authentic spirit. Many members of the post-civil rights generations have set out on an unapologetic quest to be fully and wholly who God created them to be. They are saying to the church and the world: I am who I am. Take me or leave me. Love me or hate me. No false pretense. No pretending. Just be who you are and allow me to be who I am. Has life been hard on you? Say so. Do you need a good cry? Weep openly. Are you sick? Are you weary? Are you afraid? Are you needy? Say so. And let us join in this journey together—figuring it out as we go along.

Biblical texts challenge Christians to live a life together that is authentic, honest, healing, countercultural, and bold. Most of Jesus's challenges with the Pharisees and Sadducees are disagreements over authenticity in how one lives a God-pleasing life. In the Gospel of Luke, Jesus heals a woman who was bent over for eighteen years after being inflicted by a spirit with an illness. The "church people" verbalized their anger that Jesus healed her—after all, Jesus's healing was on the Sabbath. But then Jesus challenges the gathered people: "You hypocrites! Doesn't each of you on the Sabbath untie your ox or donkey from the stall and lead it out to give it water? Then should not this woman, a daughter of Abraham, whom Satan has kept bound for eighteen long years, be set free on the Sabbath day from what bound her" (Luke 13:15-16).

In our congregations, our unyielding tradition, form, function, and our need to compete complicate and keep us from living out authentic Christian lives. We confuse church membership with Christian discipleship. We confuse tithes and offerings with dues and tips. We mistake mission for an activity or a trip rather than a way of life. German theologian Dietrich Bonhoeffer calls this "cheap grace." In *The Cost of Discipleship*, Bonhoeffer writes, "cheap grace is the preaching of forgiveness without requiring repentance, baptism without church discipline. Communion without confession. Cheap grace is grace without discipleship, grace without the cross, grace without Jesus Christ."[2] We want all of the benefits but none of the responsibility of being a part of the body of Christ. Christ demands signs of authenticity in our sanctuaries and on our subways; in our Sunday school classrooms and in our church council boardrooms; at home and at work; with the people we love and with the people we hate. To be one called Christian and one called a member of a community of faith demands tangible evidence of the presence of God in the whole of our lives. It's not enough to say you believe the Gospel of Christ; you must live it.

An Authenticity Check

The church is in need of an authenticity check, both as an institution and as a movement. The individual people of God who make up the body of Christ need an authenticity check. Congregational leaders would do well to provide opportunities for corporate and individual authenticity checkups. Corporately, are we who we are to be today for the people of God? Contextually speaking, are we doing everything we can do to make disciples of Jesus Christ for the transformation of the world? Is everything we do rooted in the biblical mandate to preach the gospel, give sight to the blind, set the captive free, and declare the year of the Lord's favor (Luke 4:18-19)? Individually, are we providing opportunities to discern: in my heart, am I who God called me to be? Am I judgmental? Am I honest? Am I kind? Do I practice forgiveness? If I need help, do I ask for it? Do I seek wise counsel? Do I set a loving example that others can follow? Do I tell the truth in love? Do I lend myself to accountability? Do I hold others accountable? John Wesley Lord, a bishop of The Methodist Church who was active in the American Civil Rights movement and who pushed for racial integration in the church, pointed out that the "Church has recruited people who had been starched and ironed before they were washed."[3] For the church, the journey to authenticity starts with a good washing!

In his 2002 book, *The Good Life*, Peter J. Gomes[4] writes of the millennial generation that they have a growing desire to right the wrongs of the parents who overcompensated in raising them. They were a generation that was returning to spiritual pursuits and a search for meaning. Raised by parents who were increasingly distracted from congregational life and family life by the pursuit of the almighty dollar and climbing the corporate ladder, this generation went to church when visiting grandparents, but not as a regular family practice. They had a lot of babysitters and gadgets to help to raise themselves. They were given things to occupy their time and distract them from missing parents. They were increasingly irritated with parents who were more concerned with career paths than call and vocation. Gomes points out that this generation of baby boomer parents were raised by the "greatest generation" that was thrifty, loyal, and commanded high levels of respect. They had strict parents and very little say in their day-to-day activities. They went to church religiously and were expected around the dinner table as the streetlights came on. The baby boomer parents granted their millennial children a lot of freedom of choice and thought; they loosened the reigns, thinking they were giving their children an easier childhood. The millennial generation, now in their thirties, is beginning to raise their own children. They continue to be the generation that demands authenticity in church and community life. They are returning to authenticity in family life, redefining the traditional definitions of family, and setting new trends in living authentic lives.

Congregations must be authentic in what they say and do. You must. It is not a choice. It is not an ideal to strive for. It is an action that you make up your mind to live into. Say what you mean and mean what you say. Walk equals talk. Word matches deed. If you say that you love, you have to love everyone—yes, everyone—yes, even them! This is hard work. This is **heart** work. Before the church attempts to be in ministry with anybody other then itself, it must work on who it is and how it acts. Congregations sing about being transformed and changed by grace in worship and fight in church council meetings. Authenticity does not teach or learn about the love of Jesus in Sunday school and then stand on the church steps and talk about what Mrs. Jones is (or is not) wearing. Authenticity does not sign up to participate in the mission project in Haiti and then frown at the person sitting in your favorite pew on Sunday morning. Authenticity does not go to church and smile on Sunday and curse the boss and coworkers at work on Monday.

Authenticity is one package. It is one image. Either Jesus has made a difference in your life or not. All or nothing. Authenticity is a lifestyle, not a momentary glimpse of vulnerabilities. *Star Wars'* Yoda might have put it best: "Do or do not. There is no try." Authenticity is a nonnegotiable. It is the major sticking point for most members of post-civil rights generations. Even Ghandi said, "I love your Christ, but I don't like your Christians. They are nothing like your Christ."

19

An Authentic Identity

What does an authentic church look like? What does a church with an authentic identity look like? Congregations that are authentic and have an authentic identity are clear, decisive, discriminating, and uncompromising about their mission. Everything they do and say is in line with and flows out of their commitment to fulfill their mission. These congregations are bold enough to say, "This is the life that God has called us to and we will not bend on it." These congregations practice congregational life in such a way that anyone who passes by or looks in can tell what is important to a specific congregation. These are the churches that have positive and definitive reputations in their communities. People can point to these congregations and say, "That's the church that (insert description)" or "Go to that church if you need (insert need)." Authentic congregations do not seek to leave anyone behind or leave anyone out; they are simply clear that they cannot be all things to all people and consequently are not a good fit for everyone. Even still, authentic congregations are among the most inclusive congregations in thought, race, age, socioeconomic status, gender, and religious background.

Congregations with an authentic identity are usually congregations with strong missional mindsets. These congregations are community and outwardly focused. These congregations are active and important participants in their community life. They focus on transformation at home—both in the pews and on the sidewalks outside of the church doors. These congregations are usually the go-to place for community gatherings and meetings such as Alcoholics Anonymous, sports programs, community financial classes, and more. People flock to these congregations in times of tragedy and for celebrations. The community already knows the church because the congregation has already invested in their lives.

Congregations that possess authentic identities are clear about their strengths and weaknesses. They celebrate their strengths, strengthen their weaknesses, and take on new opportunities. These congregations are forward thinking and creative in ministry. They take Holy Spirit-led risks and invite others along. Congregations with an authentic identity are not afraid to fail and are not afraid to share their stories. Congregations with an authentic identity share their battle scars so that others might find a place of redemption and transformation without judgment. Community members and congregation members know that they can trust the work and the word of these congregations.

Congregational leaders of these churches are community leaders—known to the school principles, coffeehouse baristas, firefighters, city council leaders, house-less community members, and restaurant servers in their communities. These leaders are clear that they are the community's pastor and not just the gathered congregation's spiritual leader. These leaders are courageous and prophetic leaders who are not afraid to speak truth to power and who hold their congregations accountable for fruitful and contagious Christian living. These congregational leaders have high expectations that there will be tangible fruit of transformed lives in their pews and communities. These congregational leaders are often criticized and yet, appear fearless. More precisely, these leaders are deeply discerning, spiritual, God-connected people who seek God in all things and who act out of the confirmation of God's word and the power of the Holy Spirit in their own lives and in the lives of the people around them.

Congregations that possess authentic identities are congregations that practice transparency as a rule in all that they do and say. In the world of the prosperity gospel and congregational leaders who possess jets and multimillion-dollar homes, the church must go the extra mile in practicing transparency with money. While millennials have been tagged the "me, me, me" generation, recent studies suggest that this is not the case. In the last two years, *The Christian Century*[5], AARP[6] and *USA Today* joined the ranks of media and study groups to challenge the preconceived notion that the millennial generation is selfish and not generous. Cara Newton of *USA Today* writes in a December 2013 article, "Millennials often require a greater degree of transparency when giving charity—57 percent reported a desire to directly see the impact of their donation, according to the Blackbaud study."[7] Thus, the issue is not the generosity of post-civil rights generations. Rather, the onus is transferred to the church to show how the money that these generations give is making a difference in the community in tangible ways. Post-civil rights generations are generous when the cause matters to them. They may hesitate to give to congregations that cannot explain where and how the building fund is used. Congregations should expect post-civil rights generations to balk at financial appeals from the pulpit that are not spiritually grounded and do not support the mission of the congregation in the community. At the end of the day, post-civil rights generations want to know that what they have given matters.

Congregations who have made a conscious decision to become a congregation with an authentic identity have not done this without cost. There will always be people who like things exactly as they are. There will be people who will disagree that the congregation does not already have an authentic identity. Still, there will be others who fight vehemently against any congregational leadership—clergy or lay—who tries to steer the congregation toward authenticity and accountability. This is not easy or people-pleasing work. This is turning over tables, enraging the Pharisees, standing against the status quo kind of work. This is countercultural work. This is authentic work. And it must be done.

Congregational Authenticity

Any congregation that launches toward the journey of authenticity must hold its members accountable for authenticity in what is said and in how words are said. In the world of e-mail, text messaging, and social media, words—their tone and their intent—are often misinterpreted. Churches are especially at risk of falling prey to this enhanced sensitivity around communication. Church visitors, community members, and members of post-civil rights generations bring a heightened sensitivity to church people and their words. Many have previously been injured by the words of church people and are prepared to be hurt again. They are used to being lied to by church people—the "I love you but..." syndrome. They are used to hearing, "I have to love you, but I don't have to like you"; "Hate the sin, not the sinner"; "We don't talk about that in church"; and "We're a friendly church (which includes the unspoken declaration) if you're just like us." None of these phrases lead to authentic relationships or opportunities for transformation in the lives of pre-disciples or striving disciples. Post-civil rights generations are predisposed to catch congregations in a lie. Authenticity demands honesty, respect, and consistent communication. I love you must mean I love you. You are welcome here must mean you are welcome here. No exceptions. No ifs, ands, or buts. Words have power and authentic words can lead to life transformation. Authentic congregations mean what they say. Their words are trustworthy and true!

Congregations launching toward authenticity must be who you say you are all the time. After all, actions speak louder than words! Members of congregations who have authentic identities must resist the temptation to be double-minded. Authenticity extends behaviors to all places and all times. If you are a people called Christian at church, you must also be one at work, at home, in traffic, in the voting booth, with finances, on social media; there is no time off. This is a heavy burden to carry. Yet, it is the fruit of the transformed life. When I was growing up, the old saints of the church used to say, "I'm not who I want to be, but thank God I'm not who I used to be!" This is a classic exclamation of sanctification—the striving of perfection in behavior and the living of a Christian life. Authentic behavior is a lifelong pursuit and commitment to always striving to do better and to be better because Christ first loved us.

Authentic congregations are called to grow people who are the whole package. Authentic congregations have attenders, members, and disciples. Yet, they expect that all attenders and members grow into multiplying disciples. Members approach church life with a sense of entitlement. They claim things like pews and rooms as their own. They pay their "dues," so they are entitled to be listened to above others and to participate in decision-making. Members approach church life as if they are to be served and to be kept happy and comfortable. Members expect benefits. On the other hand, disciples understand that they are students, learners, and contributors to a bigger picture and a greater good. Disciples take on the responsibility of understanding that "much will be demanded from everyone who has been given much."[8] Disciples seek to serve rather than to be served. Disciples understand that they are on a journey of discovery, redemption, and transformation. They do not have to have all of the answers. They do not have to be in charge all of the time. They understand that everything they have is a gift from God. Disciples seek authentic relationships with God and people. Disciples are actively traveling on a path of growth; yet they understand that growth comes in many forms and is often not predictable, linear, or consistent. Disciples trust their teacher and lean not on their own understanding. Authentic congregations are made up of disciples—often in different places on their growth journeys—but nonetheless, helping each other along.

Thou Shall Not Front

The second commandment is Thou Shall not Front. Congregations that are not frontin' and have authentic identities celebrate the processes and progresses in their congregation. There is no perfect church and there are no perfect people. Even still, congregations of authentic identities are trying. With everything they have, they are trying to be grace-filled, Holy Spirit-led, inviting, engaging, outward-focused places of honest, healing, countercultural, and bold ministry. They understand that grace is truly sufficient for everyone. They resist spiritual propaganda. They resist being all things to all people. They resist pomposity. They resist frontin'. And they proclaim to the world and their communities: You are who God made you. Given the choice to take you or leave you, we choose you. To love or hate you? We choose to love you authentically. These congregations resist false pretense and pretending. They say: Has life been hard on you? Do you need a safe place to cry? Are you sick? Are you weary? Are you afraid? Are you needy? So are we. Let us join in this journey together—figuring it out as we go along.

Covenant Practice: Authenticity

1. In your opinion, what are the marks of authentic witness and identity in your church? What is the reputation of your church in your community? In your denomination?

2. Think of a person in your congregation who might be an authentic witness. What can be learned from him or her? Why do you think he or she is an authentic witness?

3. Corporately: is our congregation who we are supposed to be to all the people of God? Is our congregation doing everything we can do to make disciples of Jesus Christ for the transformation of the world? How can we be sure that all we do is rooted in the biblical mandate to preach the gospel, give sight to the blind, set the captive free, declare the year of the Lord's favor?

4. Individually: in my heart, am I who God called me to be? Am I judgmental? Am I honest? Am I kind? Do I practice forgiveness? If I need help, do I ask for it? Do I seek wise counsel? Do I set a loving example that others can follow? Do I tell the truth in love? Do I lend myself to accountability? Do I hold others accountable in a loving and authentic way? Am I willing to make a deeper commitment to walk closer with Jesus?

Third Commandment

Thou Shall Not Trip: Discuss Taboo Subjects

Trippin': When someone is overreacting or getting all bent out of shape over something small[1]

In Numbers 13, Moses sends out twelve spies to Canaan. Moses sends one spy from each of the twelve tribes of Israel—"all the men were leaders among the Israelites."[2] Moses does not send novices. Moses does not send those who the tribes want to get rid of. Moses does not even send those who have a reason to do anything but give their very best to the mission to which they have been called. And as far as we know, none of the spies had an ulterior motive or an ax to grind with the Canaanites. Moses sends the twelve spies saying, "Go...inspect the land. What is it like? Are the people who live in it strong or weak, few or many? Is the land in which they live good or bad...camps or fortresses...rich or poor?" Moses directs the spies to "'be courageous and bring back the land's fruit'" for it was the season of the first ripe grapes.[3]

If one of the "spies" worshipped with your congregation on a Sunday morning, Wednesday night, or even Saturday night, what would they find? Would they find that the people are strong or weak, few or many? Would they say that the land in which your congregation lives is good or bad; unwalled or fortified; rich or poor? Without signage or asking, would they know that the purpose of your congregation is to make disciples of Jesus Christ for the transformation of the world? In their boldness, would they find boldness among the gathered congregation? Not only do congregations have to be authentic (chapter two), but bold.

Playing It Safe

Over and over again, church consultants, research polls, and church critics alike tell the church that boldness is one of the keys for executing transformative ministry. Boldness is one of the first steps in transformation because boldness requires a transformative step on the part of the one who seeks to be a part of another's transformation. Not even Jesus made a disciple or transformed anything or anybody without taking a bold step. To be bold is to take a risk, to step out of a comfort zone with courage and confidence. Many churches live and thrive in the "safe zone." The safe zone is a place of familiarity and it costs congregations very little to dwell there. It is a place defined by, "But we've always done it that way." It is often defined by, "Oh no, honey, we do not talk about that here," or "That is just simply inappropriate." The unspoken boundary of the safe zone is fear. Congregations will push as far as their cerebral knowledge will allow them and then they will stop because humans fear what they do not know.

Today's churches can be accused of *trippin'* because they will not push the boundaries of the safe zone. Congregations have fostered environments in which they have incubated a sensitivity and immaturity in church members. Congregations take great care to ensure that the faithful do not get their feelings hurt, in some cases by allowing them to hold congregational progress hostage. Congregations are unwilling to move beyond what is familiar in order to find and use their prophetic voice to be in conversation *with* the taboo subjects of the day. Please do not misunderstand or misinterpret what is being communicated here. Churches are good at using voices to speak at, out, and against contemporary issues. However, where congregations generally get stuck is in finding appropriate ways of seeking to discuss the taboo subjects of the day. When we speak to, out, or against an issue, we speak our opinions, our (at times bad) theology, and our emotional reactions to events, people, activities, or beliefs. When we raise our prophetic and collective voice, after consulting the Almighty God, we are enabled through the power of the Holy Spirit to be in conversation with people, beliefs, events, and activities. Conversations involving taboo subjects need to be both intentional, engaged, and active listening and intentional, careful, and prayerful speaking.

Yet, before congregations are even able to enter conversations about the taboo subjects of the day, they must be willing to engage the elephants in their own churches. Speaking in conversation with taboo subjects involves recognition and wrestling with the duplicity that is usually involved with hot button issues. Christians are called to live out a countercultural gospel. This countercultural gospel creates conflict in the body of Christ and the world. It creates a sense of tension between belief and action that often causes Christians to appear hypocritical in their responses to the prevalent social issues. All people come to the proverbial table with their own experiences, with different backgrounds, with differing theological positions, and with different expected outcomes; everyone brings his or her own baggage to the conversation that must be unloaded. Humanity speaks, hears, and lives out of its previous experiences. Racism, sexism, ageism, homophobia, plurality of religion, sacred cows, and sacred spaces are experiences that hold congregations hostage and unable to engage with post-civil rights generations. Rather, instead of focusing on "Who are your people?" post-civil rights generations challenge congregations to refocus around the question: "What has God called you to?" Understanding that this is the case, congregations must be willing to name their own elephants and unload their own baggage before they will achieve integrity in engaging in discussing taboo issues with others.

Redefining Expectations

Post-civil rights generations come to the table with a different set of tools, rules, and expectations. Members of post-civil rights generations come to the table with a different set of societal and cultural norms. From societal conditioning to educational advancement, to membership in a global community—post-civil rights generations see things through a different set of lenses than pre-civil rights generations and the civil rights generation itself. Most members of the post-civil rights generations have never been in a legally segregated classroom, workplace, restaurant, or place of leisure. By the time these generations were born, it was unlawful to have expired textbooks in their classrooms. While they may not have had access to equal number of resources (i.e., a full computer lab versus one or two computers) due to their socioeconomic status, they had access to equivalent resources as mandated by law.

The year I (Jasmine) matriculated as a kindergarten student in the Atlanta public school system, just like many other school systems around the country, our school was transitioning from teaching children to read using books like, *See Spot Run* to using computer programs like *Reader Rabbit*. As a young child, I learned to read using phonics, sight words, and games on Apple computers with my friend, Reader Rabbit. Reader Rabbit had no race, class, or preconceived notions about me, my performance, or my work ethic based on my gender, race, or class. Reader Rabbit spoke with a nondescript, yet inviting and encouraging voice. The more I worked with Reader Rabbit, the more the Rabbit adapted to my reading style and ability. Reader Rabbit lived in my school's reading (computer) lab, and he made a big deal that I was present when I logged on.

AOL, formerly America Online, launched Internet services around 1985. In 1988, it provided dial-up Internet service for personal computers. Its predecessor, Prodigy, was created in 1980. The post-civil rights generations are hard-pressed to remember a world without some kind of electronic access to resources, people, and ideas. The technology world advanced by leaps and bounds during this generation's formative years, bringing fax machines, personal computers, cell phones, graphing calculators, notebook computers, and tablets to their fingertips. Their educational opportunities literally included giving them the world—through terms abroad and foreign exchange programs. They were granted access to whatever school they could get transportation to through magnet programs and city initiatives like Atlanta's Minority to Majority program in the mid-1980s. And now, through social media, peer exchanges, and ease of travel, these generations are global citizens. There are very few matters about which the post-civil rights generations have not been exposed, educated, or informed. Yet in spite of all of this access and innovation, the church remains one of these generations' only places to experience segregation, isolation, resistance, and unwillingness to engage.

The civil rights generation raised the post-civil rights generations to be critical thinkers, to have opinions, and to use logic, deductive reasoning, and creativity to arrive at an informed answer. The "correct" answer took a backseat to the process to get to "your" answer. The church is trippin' when it comes to relating to this generation. The church wants these "out-of-the-box" individuals to fit into a mold that was created for them by generations taught to conform. While the church celebrates conformity and abiding by "your place," the post-civil rights generations are seeking congregations that are prepared to engage in difficult, long, and, often, dissonant conversations. They seek congregations who are willing to discuss the issues of importance to these generations and to speak prophetically and kindly about them. They seek congregations who will disagree with them in loving ways and who are not afraid of push back on long-held beliefs. They seek congregations who will engage in conversations rather than giving them clichéd phrases and repetitive politically correct answers.

Many of today's churches, like other congregations, cannot come to the table to discuss taboo issues because they are stuck. The traditional hang-ups like racism, sexism, economic discrimination, sexuality issues, and ageism hold congregations hostage from even beginning to discuss the taboo subjects of the day. Congregations that are still fighting church leaders about appointing female clergy to "their" church (even though, for example, The United Methodist Church started ordaining women over fifty years ago) are not prepared to engage generations that include female members who are on track to be Fortune 500 CEOs. Congregations that vehemently resist cross-racial and cross-cultural appointments (even though we desegregated churches and The United Methodist denomination over forty years ago) are not prepared to engage in conversation with generations that are culturally and ethnically diverse. While multiethnic and multicultural churches remain an enigma to many congregations, these generations are unfamiliar with the hang-ups that keep congregations debating these issues or ignoring them all together. Congregations refuse to ask the hard questions of each other: Is it our church or is it God's church? Do we love all people or do we only love the people who we know or who look like us or who make the same amount of money that we make? What are we afraid of? As long as congregations remain stuck, they remain unable to discuss taboo subjects and thereby, unable to be relevant and willing participants in transformation. If the church is interested in engaging in helpful and transformative ways, it will have to redefine its expectations and let go of its long-held presuppositions about God's people.

Stop Trippin'

Why is it important to stop trippin'? While it would be a gross miscalculation to say that members of post-civil rights generations agree on all of the taboo issues of the day, by and large, post-civil rights generations do not have the same hang-ups as the generations that have come before them. Post-civil rights generations do not want to be a part of a movement or an institution that has been paralyzed by its own fear. If congregations begin to understand that it is fear that holds them hostage, then they can understand that fear is at the root of most of the things that keep churches from being places of prophetic transformation. If we fuss about the woman pastor "they" want to send to "my" church, then we are tasked with aligning our deep gender biases with our "word" that we "love" all people. If congregations will fight a cross-racial appointment with everything that they have, even threatening to withhold financial commitments, then they must face their fear of people who do not look or act like they do. Further, fears of change, rejection, growth, the unknown, decline, and demise are all underlying and silent currents that run through reactionary and exclusive decision-making in congregations. If congregants juxtapose these fears with what we think we know and believe about God, an explosive situation ensues. Congregations must learn to turn the explosive situations into useful growth experiences. As the people of God, we must be reminded of the scripture guidance that God has not given us a spirit that is timid but one that is powerful, loving, and self-controlled![4] We must wrestle with our own demons if we are to stop trippin'!

How do congregations move forward and become safe havens for discussing taboo issues? First, congregations must let go of the things that hang them up—individually and corporately. Some things only come by prayer and fasting; letting go of deeply held beliefs that hang us up is one of those things. Only God can do the work of changing hearts and minds. Holding up the mirror to ourselves is hard and painful work. Ask God to shed light on individual and corporate opportunities for growth and change. Ask for forgiveness of past actions, words, beliefs that do not line up with Christ's command to love our neighbor. Pray "breath prayers,"[5] quick and frequent prayers that you can say in one breath, as a reminder that you are on a journey of transformation. Expect change in yourself before demanding it from others.

Next, congregations must learn to face our own conflicts in light of our own experiences. How is it that a gathering of Christians that sings, "They will know we are Christian by our love," can oppose health care for all people? How is it that Christians can openly oppose homosexuality when the church has long turned a blind eye to its beloved and "anointed" gay choir director? How can congregations pray for peace in one breath and, in another, urge congressional leaders and the White House to spend more money on war than on education? What about the conflict of well-meaning Christians who, in the name of homeland security, encourage funding international regimes that persecute their people, but oppose open paths to immigration so that these might have a chance at a better life? How do we talk openly about

37

fidelity in marriage and gossip so that Mrs. Johnson does not hear the news that everybody else already knows—Mr. Johnson's mistress is pregnant. What about telling Mrs. Smith to go back home to her abuser-husband and encouraging her to be a "godly" wife in an effort to curb his temper? The Bible challenges us to remove the plank in our eyes before trying to remove the speck in another's eye. Do we believe that all people are God's people? Do we really believe that all people are created in the image and love of God? Do we really believe that all people deserve the abundance of life that God promises? In our challenge with negotiating duplicity, Christians foster hypocrisy, which, in turn, disqualifies congregations from being able to engage in fruitful conversations about taboo issues. The reality is that many congregations will not come to agreement in all of the taboo issues of the day. Christian history proves this—denominations and congregations split because groups of people cannot discern the will of God in the same way. Yet, congregations can challenge themselves to come to agreement in how to move forward together in Christian love and unity. In facing their own conflict, congregations open the door for post-civil rights generations to engage in fruitful conversation and can provide models for society about how to move forward together in light of conflict and disagreement.

Next, congregations must learn to be present in the taboo issues. From abortion rights to gun control; urban violence to teen suicides; homosexuality to any discussion of sexuality at all; classism to racism; ageism to sexism; educational opportunities to educational inadequacies; power to politics—the church must step up, step into, and be prepared to engage in conversations about the practical issues that matter in real life to real people. Engaging in conversation with the taboo subjects of the day demands more than words; it requires action. The post-civil rights generations have long grown weary of empty words. How is your congregation engaged in your community around these issues? Is your image in relation to these issues an image of love or of hate? How do you intend for your image to be perceived? How is your image actually perceived?

Next, as the body of Christ, transparency, understanding, and acceptance must become our rule rather than our exception. Understanding and acceptance are not the same as agreement. Rather, transparency, understanding, and acceptance are guiding principles for respect and mutuality in living life together and in entering into conversations with post-civil rights generations and each other. If we learn to say, "Help me understand..." rather than pronouncing judgment on a person or situation out of our own experience, we are more likely to open doors for conversation rather than closing doors in perceived judgment. The church must learn to coexist in the reality of society—even if we do not agree with the actions of some of our brothers and sisters. After all, it is not our responsibility to place judgment or even to presume what God's judgment might be; God reserves that right.

The younger members of the post-civil rights generations celebrate individualism and celebrate that God created each individual with unique personalities and gifts. They grew up observing grandparents, parents, and older siblings who were guided and restricted by unspoken societal rules that make no sense to them. Therefore, they have set out to be distinct individuals—not conforming to the status quo; rather, challenging it and setting up a new way of being in the world. If we think theologically about it, this is a gift to our society and to our churches. The Bible and church history books are full of individuals who stood out of the norm and shaped our biblical and theological history because of it. In Numbers, Caleb's boldness allowed him to stand outside of the majority report and it changed the course of Israelite history. Congregations must learn to foster and nurture people who will stand up and give the minority report.

Even still, in order to do this, congregations must stop trippin'! Congregations that dare to set young people free to create ministry opportunities in which people can grow fully into being whom God created them to be may discover life-giving gifts among them. There are congregations among us who are doing this work well. They have community-based ministries that seek to serve beyond their comfort zones. These congregations deeply understand and believe that they exist for the least, the last, the lost, and the lowly. They fund ministry opportunities that they do not fully understand; yet, they see the fruit of their labor and trust God in the process.

It seems that taboo is the name of the game these days. People maintain a love-hate relationship with the hot-button and lightening rod issues of the day. People are either conservative or liberal; we've forgotten that there is a middle way. In the Wesleyan tradition, of which I am a part, our founder, John Wesley, encouraged and usually landed in the *via media,* the middle way. Wesley usually landed in the middle of radical and opposing poles and found a middle way. I wonder what it would look like if congregations and individuals sought the *via media,* the middle way. Pre-civil rights generations were right: you often do catch more flies with honey. Yet, post-civil rights generations understand this: when you are raised in an environment where people look, speak, feel, learn, and grow differently, disagreement with or not understanding a lifestyle choice does not automatically breed judgment. Rather, it presents an opportunity to seek understanding. Post-civil right generations understand that acceptance is not the same as agreement and press on in relationships despite differences in belief or opinion.

In the Civil Rights South, it was often the church that was the prophetic voice in society. Church leaders of both races like Rev. Dr. Martin Luther King Jr.; Rev. Dr. Joseph Lowery; and United Methodist bishops Bevel Jones and Woodie White led the way in working against the law of the land at the time. Culture (and some church leaders) said that blacks were less than human. Prophetic and progressive church leaders said that all people are of sacred worth and deserve to be treated as such. Both sides used the Bible to make their case. Eventually, society and law yielded to the leading of those prophetic voices. Today, the church either remains largely silent or speaks with voices of judgment and condemnation. And yet, the church seems surprised when things happen without it and in spite of it. The church has marginalized its own voice by losing its "street cred" (creditability with the masses) by showing that its words rarely match its actions and even more rarely model the teachings of Jesus. Jesus challenged followers to be in the world but not of the world. Yet, the church has set up an "us" versus "them" relationship with secular society.

Post-civil rights generations struggle to understand the perceived adversarial relationship between the church and the world.

If the church resists dealing with the reality of current culture, where are the post-civil rights generations to gain guidance and find models of compassion? Instead of turning to the church, post-civil rights generations are turning to television, websites, online discussion forums, blogs, social media outlets, and peer groups for a belief system. As long as good church people continue to trip over taboo subjects, younger generations will turn away and continue to view and condemn the church as irrelevant, hypocritical, and inaccessible.

One of the ways congregations regain their "street cred" with post-civil rights generations is to willingly and honestly engage in open conversations about the taboo subjects that matter. Open conversations are best modeled, not demanded. Church people must first learn to listen to their brothers and sisters sitting in the pews with them before they can seek to listen to anyone else. Listen, listen, listen! Listen without judgment or fear. Listen without reacting negatively; yet, be engaged. As the Prayer of St. Francis says, seek to understand, rather than to be understood.

One practical way to tackle the taboo subjects is to engage in small-group studies that challenge and stretch your congregation. Many congregations configure small groups by affinity groups. What would happen if less like-minded people studied the Bible together for guidance around contemporary issues and learned to listen to each other, be challenged by each other and by the countercultural gospel of Christ, and grow together in Christ. Sermon series on taboo subjects are courageous ways to break into churchwide discussions on the taboo issues of the day if they encourage flexibility and movement in the way people think about and approach the issues. Town hall style meetings to educate and discuss issues in a safe space with predefined and communicated ground rules to hold congregations accountable for mutual respect in words and actions have proven productive in some settings—especially when talking about important community issues. Host community events that invite your community into the church doors. If hosted in a hospitable way, these events can portray to the community that you do indeed exist for them and that you want to be in relationship with them.

Thou Shall not Trip

The third commandment is Thou Shall not Trip. If congregations are to follow the commandment not to trip, they must model conversations and behaviors that are guided by the Holy Spirit and by the fruit of the Spirit. Congregations must hold each other accountable for actions, reactions, and words, especially when they do not model Christ to our communities. Congregations must lean toward holy boldness instead of timid blandness, remembering that being lukewarm is condemned in Revelation 3:16. The people called Christians must seek to understand, rather than be understood, learning to listen and respond with compassion. Congregations must relinquish fear for engagement with the taboo issues. Thou shall not trip!

Following the directions of the Lord, Moses handpicked the spies he sent to Canaan. God told Moses to send the leaders and he followed through. Moses directed the spies to be bold. When the spies returned, they returned to share their report in front of not only Moses, but also Aaron and all the congregations of the Israelites in the wilderness. Most of the leader-spies returned with fearful reports. Caleb spoke up with a bold report to move forward. What will it be for you? For your congregation? Will you remain where you are—stuck, defeated, and dying? Will you be held back by the naysayers? Or will you take the challenge to be bold, move forward, and engage the taboo issues? Will you be the one to stop the trippin'?

Covenant Practice: Be Bold

1. Read Numbers 13:25-30. Where you are in this story? Are you a leader? Are you a part of the congregation that receives the report? Are you like Caleb—bold enough to stand apart from the crowd?

2. Who are the Calebs among you? Who has the ability to lead your church in engaging the taboo subjects in your community? Make a list.

3. What are the taboo subjects in your congregation? What issues are just too hot to talk about?

4. What are the tangible ways your congregations can engage the taboo issues? How will you engage in conversations with—not at or against?

Fourth Commandment

Thou Shall Check Yourself before You Wreck Yourself:
Provide Inclusive Worship and Bible Study

You better check yourself before yo wreck yo self
Cos I'm bad for your health[1]

— *"Check Yo Self" by Ice Cube*

A congregation taking advice from an artist like Ice Cube, probably seems far-fetched. In this instance, congregations would do well to heed the words from Ice Cube to "check themselves before they wreck themselves." In other words, congregations need to watch what they say and do or they may not like the consequences. We believe this is especially true regarding worship and Bible study with post-civil rights generations. If congregations simply continue to do the same things or try to tweak the same thing to look new, then they are going to wreck themselves.

45

In Numbers 14:4, the Israelites wreck themselves. It reads, "And they said to each other, 'We should choose a leader, and go back to Egypt.'" We learn in Numbers 14:1 that the gathered Israelite tribes do not like the report from the spies about the giants and fear for their lives. They start complaining against God and Moses. The complaining culminates in Numbers 14:4 with the Israelites seeking to choose a new leader to return them to slavery in Egypt. Wow! The Israelites were in Egypt for 430 years (Exod 12:40) and enslaved for most of that time. Yet the majority of the nation was willing to go back into bondage because they feared the report of the spies who said the land was full of giants. The Israelites were willing to wreck themselves over a report from humans and to ignore what God told them. We can just imagine many of you nodding your head saying, "That is crazy!" Well, many of our congregations are not much better. They would rather force post-civil rights generations to fit into a square hole than to seriously engage them and move toward a new future in God. Talk about wrecking yourself! In this chapter we will continue helping congregations to be bold by disrupting conventional thinking.

Wreck Yourself

A pastor who wishes to remain anonymous told me this story about a Bible study aimed at the hip-hop generation.[2] The pastor talked about successfully starting a Bible study that engaged younger individuals. Those responsible for starting the Bible study were even successful in getting these young adults to come to the church. Sadly, when the hip-hop generation started showing up the drama started. Some of the more seasoned members started complaining about those kind of folk coming into the church. They "strongly encouraged" the pastor to stop the study. The pastor tried to reason with the seasoned members but finally gave in and stopped the study. This is not where the story ends.

The pastor happened to walk by the sanctuary one evening and saw one of the young men in the back watching choir practice. The pastor greeted the young man and asked how things were going. The young man asked the pastor, "Why don't we have Bible study anymore?" The young man talked about how he looked forward to it. The pastor struggled to find words that would be honest and not hurtful. Finally ended up saying something like not everyone was committed to the success of the study. It was the last time the young man ever came to church! The church just wrecked itself!

One of the challenges some congregations face is they explicitly and implicitly state they do not want those kind of folk. You know the kind of folk I am talking about, the ones seeking a deeper relationship with Jesus. The ones coming with an expectation that something transformational can happen. Some congregations do not want those kind of folk. God forbid those kind of folk find their way to the church. We would never admit to preventing individuals from having a relationship with Jesus. Instead, we claim we do not want those folks tatted all up and down their bodies, because they seem suspicious. We do not want those individuals with that strange haircut, because that is not very becoming on a young lady or man. The truth is, those folk are individuals who are different from us and we are often unwilling to go to them or to let them into our space.

Interestingly, Jesus was dealing with this same issue during his time. In Matthew 9: 9-13, we read about the call of Matthew. Jesus is walking along and calls Matthew, a tax collector, to follow him. Not only does Jesus call Matthew, he goes the next step and eats with Matthew and his former colleagues, other tax collectors. The Pharisees did not think it was appropriate for someone of Jesus's ilk to eat with tax collectors. They ask Jesus's disciples why their teacher did such a thing. Jesus responds in Matt 9:12-13a (CEB), "'Healthy people don't need a doctor, but sick people do. Go and learn what this means: *I want mercy and not sacrifice.*'"

Some may be wondering how this applies to today. Think about it. The Pharisees are a part of the religious establishment. They are concerned that everything is done decently and orderly by those connected to the synagogue. Certainly no one connected to the synagogue would eat with those people, tax collectors. No legitimate teacher would call a tax collector to be one of his disciples. Jesus did eat with those people and Jesus did call Matthew to be one of his disciples.

Some in the church today are similar to the Pharisees in not believing that everyone is suited for their congregation. For example, if your congregation is unwilling to seek those in the post-civil rights generations or to invite them into your church, then your congregation is behaving like the Pharisees who did not want those individuals who didn't fit a certain mold. In the example above of some in the congregation asking the pastor to stop the Bible study, we clearly see Pharisaic-like behavior. Some in the congregation, like the Pharisees, developed an attitude that one who is "holy" should know better than associating with people who are not like us. I am sure those opposed to the individuals coming are asking, "Why would the pastor expect those individuals to become disciples?" The rest of us should be answering, "Why not!" Unfortunately, we suspect that there are too many congregations wrecking themselves in this way.

In the Matthew 9: 9-13 text, Jesus shines a light on how developing an "us versus them" attitude leads to wrecking one's self. It is easy to pick on the Pharisees because they are often the target of Jesus's teaching. The reality is, the Pharisees are like many of us in the congregation today doing the best we can to keep the church moving. The truth is, the Pharisees, in their thinking, were only trying to seek what was best for the religious establishment. It certainly was not eating with tax collectors who were taking money from the people. While the Pharisees may not have been trying to set up an "us versus them" scenario, that is exactly what happened in the way they were living out their faith.

Jesus disrupts the Pharisees' understanding of living out their faith by challenging the "us versus them" scenario. Jesus does not buy into stereotypes or demonizing and eats with those who are considered not fit by the religious establishment. By eating with them, Jesus gets to have conversations and hear their perspectives and not just what others say about them. By eating with them, Jesus gets to hear about their beliefs and not just what others are saying about them. Jesus disrupts the dichotomy being created by the religious establishment toward those who seem unfit.

When congregations are at their best, they should be disrupting "us versus them" scenarios. Instead of buying into stereotypes about post-civil rights generations, congregations should be engaging them in dialogue. Instead of talking about what we think post-civil rights generations believe, we should talk with them about their beliefs. Congregations cannot buy into the dichotomies that are wrecking us and keeping the post-civil rights generations from fully engaging us.

Practically speaking, this means that we cannot simply determine what is right for the post-civil rights generations in worship or for Bible study. Like Jesus we have to have a conversation with them about what makes sense. We believe a part of the reason that the Pharisees are so upset with Jesus is he is regarded as a teacher, but is acting like one who has no authority. Jesus did not make the tax collectors come to him, but he went to one of their houses and ate (Matt 9:10). It is one thing to eat with those who are unfit and quite another to go into their domain. Jesus went to their domain.

The tax collectors and others knew Jesus was serious about wanting to engage them in conversation. Too many times when we want to engage the post-civil rights generations we expect them to come to the church. That is worth repeating! Too many times when we want to engage the post-civil rights generations we expect them to come to the church. The conversation has to take place on our domain.

This attitude carries over in terms of worship and Bible studies. Worship has to be at the church. Bible study has to be at the church. Everything is focused on them coming to us. Unfortunately, as we pointed out earlier in this chapter, even when they

2095 9 8

do come and do not look like us we want them to leave. On the one hand, congregations push and push to get the post-civil rights generations to come to them. On the other hand, congregations want those coming to look and act just like them. Some congregations not only set an expectation of the post-civil rights generations coming to them. They run away those who do not fit a particular mold. These congregations are wrecking themselves.

Too many congregations are wrecking themselves because they are behaving like the Pharisees in not seeking the post-civil rights generations in genuine ways. The expectation is for those in the post-civil rights generations to come dressed and looking like us, to like our worship experience that may have no meaning for them, and to participate in our Bible studies, but being careful not to talk too much. We think it is time that these congregations check themselves.

Check Yourself

In Matthew 9: 9-13, Jesus gives us clues on how we can check ourselves. By checking ourselves we mean refocusing on the gospel and not our own ambitions.[3] When we wreck ourselves, we are being pulled away from the gospel. It is in checking ourselves that we return to the gospel and its meaning for our lives. The first clue Jesus gives us is that you cannot engage those different from you by staying locked up in your building. Matthew 9:9 begins by stating, "Jesus was walking." Jesus was not simply sitting at the synagogue waiting for Matthew and his colleagues to find him. Jesus was out walking looking for them. Sitting inside the walls of our congregations and talking about the absence of the post-civil rights generations *ad nausem* is not the solution. We need to get out and walk!

We can already hear the protest. Our congregation is too old to go out. There are no post-civil rights generations in our neighborhood. These are just a few of the common excuses given. We are not suggesting that someone put their health at risk by going out of the church, but we are suggesting the need to genuinely engage the post-civil rights generations. For example, a small congregation with about twenty-five in worship and an average age of seventy-five was complaining about not having any younger individuals. The truth was, five or six younger folk were connected to the congregation. A couple of those connected were the grandchildren of worship attendees and the others were friends brought by the grandchildren.

While those in worship could not get out, they had individuals coming to them. They did not have any conversations with these individuals about their beliefs or ideas for a deeper engagement in worship. They acted like those five or six were invisible. There are some congregations who truly have no one coming under the age of seventy. Some congregations are like the one in the example and ignoring those who are coming and not engaging them in deep conversation. The possibility of transformation is right in front of the congregation, but they have not started a dialogue. Jesus did not start big, but started by calling Matthew.

The point is, even those who cannot physically walk around the neighborhood are often able to engage in dialogue if they open their eyes to the possibilities. The same is true for the comment no young folk live in our neighborhood. Is it that no young folk are in the neighborhood or none whom we know? A certain vulnerability required in ministry is getting out of our comfort zones and meeting others. If we are only looking for what is familiar, then we will never see with new eyes. Jesus teaches us to check ourselves by opening ourselves up to new possibilities and not staying with the familiar.

The next clue Jesus gives us in checking ourselves is his willingness to do things outside of the congregation. In Matthew 9:10 it states, "While Jesus was having dinner at Matthew's house..." Returning to vulnerability, too often in congregations we want those outside to take all the risk. Jesus truly was an advocate for NSFC in his willingness to be vulnerable. Jesus knew that the word would get out that he was eating with tax collectors and others considered unfit. Jesus knew that he was going against the norm in what he was doing. Jesus did it anyway! Jesus's willingness to be vulnerable and not getting caught up in what others were thinking and saying set up a possibility for connecting with outsiders.

Are we willing to disrupt conventional thinking like Jesus to engage in deep conversations on the turf of the post-civil rights generations? The text does not tell us what Jesus and the others were talking about in the house, but we can imagine that the tax collectors and others were excited to be taken seriously. The text does not tell us how many were in the house. We have to be willing to keep engaging and not give up even when numbers are not off the charts. For instance, one place where disrupting conventional thinking is required is campus ministry. Campus ministry is often very challenging because students are constantly turning over and commitment by students can be low. Too often congregations near colleges and universities get excited about reaching out, but run out of steam after awhile when participation drops.

This is where we really have to be Jesus's disciples and keep the faith. We cannot get hung up on numbers all the time, and remember, where two or three are gathered, Jesus is with us. A willingness to keep going and engaging the one or two who may show up is important. At times congregations will get out and try something, but when participation drops, give up. If we are serious about engaging the post-civil rights generations, then we cannot give up.

A part of disrupting conventional thinking is knowing we may be the only ones doing it for a season. We want to be clear that this does not mean that a ministry should just keep doing the same thing for the sake of doing it. Evaluating and making changes are crucial as things develop. Jesus does this when he goes out by altering his approach based on the context. For example, Jesus does not go to the Samaritan woman's house, but meets her at the well. We also need to alter our approach based upon context. The key point for congregations is a willingness to disrupt conventional thinking by going into someone else's domain and not expecting them to come to us. Remember, it is about checking yourself!

The final clue for checking ourselves is found in Matthew 9:13a, where Jesus states, "I desire mercy not sacrifice." This is a powerful statement by Jesus that should make all of us reconsider our motives. What is it that is really behind what we are doing in worship and Bible study? A pastor of a congregation wanted to get the younger folk more involved in worship. The pastor called a meeting to facilitate the younger folk taking a more active role and not just a backseat. For the most part the meeting went well until a comment was made, "The younger people need to sing serious music and not that stuff they like."

No one said anything during the meeting, but the damage was done as soon as the words were spoken. The music the younger folk sing is not serious and as a result should not be taken seriously. Certainly the pastor's intentions were for an honest and fruitful dialogue that would enhance worship. The younger folk attending, however, could walk away from the meeting thinking the motive was to alter the music they sing during worship. This was not the intended takeaway, but became the takeaway.

Jesus's words about mercy should be a check for those of us in congregations to remember God's grace. The person making the comment probably did not intend any harm, but the reality is, the remark points to younger folk sacrificing their musical interest to satisfy the establishment. Jesus flips the script and says the establishment needs to have mercy and not desire sacrifice. The point is that mercy enables us to move beyond like and dislike to an understanding of focusing on God. Sacrifice in the way Jesus is using it in this text is not about one side having to fit in or give in to the wishes of the other.

If congregations are seeking sacrifice from the post-civil rights generations, then they will continue to stay away from the church. If congregations are extending mercy, then opportunities are available for real conversation. Jesus was telling the Pharisees and us that we need more mercy and less sacrifice if we are going to check ourselves. Mercy is invitational and encourages dialogue. Jesus's approach to the tax collectors and others was one of mercy; this should also be our approach toward others.

The Matthew 9:13 text makes it clear that we need to check ourselves by walking, doing things away from the church, and showing mercy. It is when we check ourselves that we are encouraging a dialogue and not dictating to others. What we can learn from Jesus is the importance of remaining true to the gospel while encouraging a conversation with others who are not a part of the establishment. To do so, we have to constantly check ourselves.

Thou Shall Check Yourself before You Wreck Yourself

The fourth commandment is Thou Shall Check Yourself before You Wreck Yourself. Ice Cube was not thinking about the church when he spit the words to this hit, but the words apply to the church. Too many congregations are wrecking themselves because they are behaving like the Pharisees. They do not want to go out and often prevent people from coming into the congregation. Talk about a double whammy! Jesus encourages us to think and act differently. Jesus encourages us to check ourselves by doing those things that will create conversations with the post-civil rights generations. You do not have to be an Ice Cube fan, but you should be on the path of discipleship and this means checking yourself before wrecking yourself in reaching out to post-civil rights generations.

Covenant Practice: Disrupt Conventional Thinking

1. Read Matthew 9:9-13 and pray for guidance.

2. Make a list of the characteristics you believe that Jesus would want in a church. Compare your list with other people's. How does your church compare?

3. What are some ways in which your congregation might be wrecking itself?

4. What are some practical things your congregation can do to start checking itself? Whose job should this be? How often should the congregation evaluate itself?

5. Who in your congregation can be in dialogue with post-civil rights generations during the next six months about worship or a Bible study? How will the conversation illustrate mercy?

Fifth Commandment

Thou Shall Learn How We Roll: Create New Entry Points

How I roll: A justification for how someone behaves[1]

In the late 1990s, many mainline congregations subscribed to a church growth strategy, which many referred to as "Worship Plus Two." It was a belief that if congregations could get new members to attend and participate in worship services plus two other congregational opportunities such as Sunday school, choir, small groups, outreach ministries, women's ministries, and so on, then those new members would "stick." If new people to congregations would participate in worship plus two, you were well on your way to making new disciples. Many congregations experienced exponential growth using the worship-plus-two model. Today, many congregations still create, staff, and model ministry opportunities based on this premise. However, some church leaders, who once experienced growth using this model, are forced to assess why the worship-plus-two model is not as effective as it once was for their congregations.

The Israelites are forced to make a similar assessment of the report of the spies in Numbers 14:1-4. The majority of the Israelites go with the majority assessment. The assumption by the Israelites assembled was that numbers matter. Sometimes we begin with faulty assumptions. Congregations subscribing to the worship-plus-two model are doing the same thing. This chapter picks up from chapter four and helps us to understand how post-civil rights generations are encouraging new ways of engaging the church differently through various entry points.

The older model was based on one major assumption: worship is the primary entry point for new people to congregations. While this is not a bad assumption, it may not be as accurate as it once was. Shifts in societal beliefs have left unchurched and de-churched populations skeptical of congregations. While there was a time when the church was the center of community, civic, and spiritual life, this is no longer true. Communities used to depend on local congregations to connect them to one another and to provide a sense of grounding in their lives. Most people felt comfortable walking in the front doors of whatever denominational church they were raised in on Sunday mornings and putting down roots in that congregation. They did this through worshipping on Sunday mornings.

The Sunday morning worship experience has been a dependable activity in many communities. Most people who are new to a community know that they can walk into a church around 10 or 11 a.m. and there will be people gathered in a big room with music and a pastor. They will probably see their neighbors, their doctors, their teachers, and their civic leaders there as well.

However, the Sunday morning worship experience has become a complicated and loaded gathering. Sunday mornings remain the most segregated hours in American society. Instead of churches being primarily defined by their theological holdings, they are first described by their racial makeup. Next by their primary social economic status. Then by their political leaning. And eventually, someone might mention that they believe in and worship Jesus. What was once a forgone conclusion and habit—that people worship in communities on Sunday—is now an anxiety-producing, complex navigation to decipher whether or not the people gathered in a building that says "church" on the sign are actual practicing Christians striving to be like Jesus.

Historically, churches have tended to invest most of their programming resources—people, time, energy, money—in Sunday worship experiences. In referring to Sunday morning worship, I once heard a worship professor say, "One shot and you're done. You only get one chance to do it right. Make an impression. Give them something to remember. You have to give them a reason to come back." No pressure, worship planners. You only have one chance to make a good impression on first-time visitors because your only point of engagement with them is when they walk through the sanctuary doors.

This new reality complicates and dilutes the worship-plus-two model. As more people are hesitant to walk into worship experiences and engage Christian communities through that traditional entry point, the previously assumed primary entry point loses its effectiveness as a point of initial engagement. As more people worship online, on television, or plan to avoid worship all together, how will the church connect new people into other points of connection in the church as suggested by the worship-plus-two model?

All Else Has Failed. Now What?

The worship-plus-two model only works when people value worship as a commitment worth their time and energy. They must regard the worship experience as the primary entry point into the life of the church. If these assumptions don't ring true, the model falls apart and the church is left wondering why they are not growing and attracting new people. People blame the style of worship, the music, the preacher, the worship time, the paint color in the sanctuary, the length of the worship experience, and whatever else seems convenient. Yet, it may not be any of those things. In fact, while worship can always stand an effectiveness assessment—after all, as Wesleyans, we are not yet perfect—worship may not be broken. Rather, the model and its assumptions are what need adjustment.

Christian theologians define worship in a variety of ways and as having many different aspects. In his classic book, *Introduction to Christian Worship*, James F. White points to Martin Luther's definition as "one of the most attractive definitions of Christian worship... 'that nothing else be done in it than that our Lord Himself talk to us through His holy word and that we, in turn, talk to him in prayer and song of praise.'"[2] Justo L. González defines worship as "an act of God's grace... celebrat[ing] God's graceful acceptance of ourselves;... offered unacceptable gifts, trusting that the same grace that has accepted us will accept them."[3] Edward P. Wimberly defines corporate worship as "an act of people in a local church as they...give praise to God for being drawn into God's story...hav[ing] found meaning and purpose in their lives."[4] Melva Wilson Costen describes corporate worship as a "gather[ing]...to be spiritually fed by the Word of God! In response to God's call and by God's grace, communities of faith gather to affirm God's providence and power. "[5] Most communities of faith, however, define worship by describing what happens in worship. They may offer a list of actions: we sing, we praise, we pray, we give, we hear from God through the sermon. They also define the worship event by what does and does not happen there saying things such as: "The Holy Spirit was with us." "The preacher really had a great sermon!" "I hope they don't sing that song anymore!" For many communities of faith worship is defined inwardly and not outwardly.

Congregations who are engaging or long to engage in effective worship practices are constantly asking: Who is worship for? Who does worship serve? The process for gathering answers to these questions cannot be insulated. Worship committees shouldn't have the only say in defining "engaging and inspiring worship."[6] Rather, effective worship exploration inquires of the people who are not in worship. It seeks to understand why they do not worship with you. Regardless of how one defines worship, Christians agree that worship is dependent and primarily hinges on a relationship with God and is the work of the Holy Spirit and the gathered people.

Is worship the best point of entry for an outsider? If we understand corporate worship as a relational and responsive gathering, then why do we invite people who have no relationship with God or context for church/religion to worship first—as the primary entry point to Christianity and to church? Would that not be like asking a stranger to jump in headfirst to one of our most sacred and long-held family traditions that only our family members would understand? If we believe that worship is undergirded by an understanding that people worship because they are in relationship with Christ and others, why would we put all of our proverbial eggs in the worship basket as the primary mechanism through which to connect people to Christ and church?

Worship as the primary entry point was the strongest mechanism through which to engage new people in new faith communities when church attendance and Christianity was a foregone conclusion in our communities. Today, Christianity is an option among many options for living out life. With growing numbers of young people who have no religious affiliation and no previous exposure to Christianity or faith communities, the church must find a different and more familiar way to engage post-civil rights generations.

Alternate Entry Points

If worship is no longer the strong and primary entry point that it once was, the church is challenged to find and offer multiple and alternate entry points that allow new people to engage in Christian discipleship in the context of communities of faith. Based on a congregation's specific context, churches and congregational leaders would do well to consider mission and social activism; small groups; preschools and after-school ministries; age-level ministries; affinity groups; and web-based, social, and digital engagements as strong alternate entry points.

Missions and Social Activism Ministries have become the most native and accessible entry points for post-civil rights generations primarily because of the educational orientation of these generations. Most secondary schools, colleges, and universities require their graduates to complete ongoing community service hours as a part of their academic program. Most members of post-civil rights generations cannot meet the requirements for graduation unless they learn how to serve others. For the church, this means that they know how to serve and they seek opportunities to serve in their communities. Service allows them to meet one of the primary longings in life, to have and add meaning in and to the world. Congregations that view and create mission ministries as primary entry points to the faith community and to discipleship create an organic and familiar place of connection and belonging for post-civil rights generations who are much more likely to wake up to build a Habitat House than they are to wake up for worship.

Small-Group Ministries as primary entry points for post-civil rights generations acknowledge generational yearnings to be in meaningful relationships with people. Small groups provide grounding for life purpose and are fertile breeding ground for building relationships with new people, in new places, often at times when members of post-civil rights generations are outgrowing their old networks and relationships. Yet, these young people are not always aware that this is what is happening. Small groups help provide an understanding that as life changes, people change and grow. They also help young people understand that they are not alone in experiencing life change and maturity in personality and relationships. Small groups provide built-in safe spaces to grow, change, learn, evolve, and connect with God and people. When offered during nontraditional times and in nontraditional spaces, small groups provide nonthreatening and convenient entry places for new people to enter faith communities.

For the middle and older of the post-civil rights generation members, **Preschools and After-School Ministries** can provide good, safe programs, which are perceived as hard to come by in today's society. Preschool families become tight-knit communities in and of themselves and when engaged correctly and lovingly, see the church to which the preschool is connected as an additional place of connection and belonging for their family. At a time when many young families do not live near their families of origin and lack a great deal of family support, there is an overwhelming need to have a place of belonging for their children and for themselves. These ministries do not work as good entry points if they are simply tenants in a church facility. These ministries must be the work and commitment of the congregation and must be deeply connected to the congregational and community life of the church.

Solid, nurturing, integrated **Age-Level Ministries** signal to parents that the congregation understands that parenting is hard and that the church can and wants to help. They also signal to students that they are important and that they are not alone in navigating the challenges of growing up. They signal to young adults that the church wants to be a partner in helping to navigate growth and lifestyle changes. They signal to older adults that you are not forgotten and alone as you move into new and uncharted stages of life. Age-level ministries for children, youth, young adults, and older adults that do not stand alone but rather, are integrated into the full life of a congregation become sustaining, supporting, and directing entry points for new people.

Affinity Groups ask the question, "What is missing in our community?" Affinity groups differ from small groups in that they are created around a perceived and/or real need—generally around a shared interest, idea, or belief. Affinity groups are gatherings such as parenting groups, scrapbooking groups, yoga classes, classes that help with individual or family finances. When a church discovers what community need it can help fill, it then can create affinity groups that fills a gap for the people in the community. While small groups are generally inwardly focused because they focus on developing disciples and congregational connections to God and people, affinity groups are intended to be community-based, open, and always invitational. Affinity groups are not intended to last forever; rather, they ebb and flow based on community need.

When congregations invest in **Web, Social Media, Digital Engagement,** they create congregational entry points that take the pressure off people to interface with communities before they are ready or able. Websites are the new front door of a church. If your church's website is out-of-date, difficult to navigate, lacking pertinent information like worship times, a physical address, and good contact information, you might as well not have a website at all. If you do not have a website at all, the majority of potential visitors are likely to cross your congregation off of their list without even trying you out.

Most congregations confuse the website for the newsletter. Websites are to be invitational and not informational—providing a digital version of your church's "welcome" desk. Invitational websites are clean, easy to navigate, and answer the questions that everyone else already knows the answers to like: Where do I park? What do I wear? What time should I arrive? Who will I see when I get there? What will I experience? Which door do I come in? Is there a nursery/children's ministry/youth ministry? Are children welcome in worship? Who are the pastoral and lay leaders? Am I really welcome? Does it matter to you if I come or not?

Via the website and social media platforms, congregations can provide devotional material, online Bible studies, and access to worship opportunities that allow potential congregants to join the community long before they engage with the people of the congregation. Through social media, congregants and pastors can engage in a more informal basis, allowing people to see their humanity and willingness to be in relationship with them. By providing flexible opportunities to participate in the life of the church, congregations signal to their connecting community that they want them to be a part of the congregation even if they cannot be or are not yet willing to be physically a part of the faith community. Congregations that provide digital engagement on salient issues help potential congregations understand what they believe and provide undergirding in turbulent times. In social media, web presences and digital engagement, congregations provide "connection" and accountability, which allows hesitant connectors to feel as if they belong before they step foot on the property or participate in any of the congregational ministries.

Break the Rules

New disciples will not be made en masse if congregations stand by and passively expect people to walk through the front doors of the church on Sunday morning. Churches must break the traditional "rules" of evangelism and provide multiple, creative, and easily accessible entry points to faith communities. The focus of the congregation must move beyond membership to discipleship. Some people will never become "members" of congregations. Yet, they will grow into contagious and committed disciples of Jesus Christ. The task of the congregation is to reduce the revolving-door effect which supports a steady entry and exit of a congregation. Churches experiencing the revolving-door effect may experience a steady stream of first-time visitors but very few visitors who "stick." Moving from a revolving-door effect to sustainable engagement of disciples requires multiple entry points.

Once new people travel through an entry point, they often experience information overload. In the name of welcome and excitement, congregations overload new people with information on the many ministries of the church and many activities to attend. Moving our focus with new people from information overload to transformational engagement, allows new people to find their place in the congregation without the overwhelming feeling in the name of hospitality.

Thou Shall Learn How We Roll

The fifth commandment is Thou Shall Learn How We Roll. In Numbers, Caleb and the minority reporters break with the status quo and it paid off for a whole nation of people for many generations. If congregations are willing to move beyond seeing the worship experience as the only and primary entry point of new people in the life of the church and create new and multiple places of entry which are based on community need and behaviors, many new disciples might be made for Christ and congregations just might transform their communities in the name of Jesus! This is how congregations should roll!

Covenant Practice: Various Entry Points

1. What would you identify as the primary entry point(s) to your faith community?

2. Are the primary entry points of your congregation intentionally designed to reach different types of people in different stages in life? How so?

3. How could you start or transform the following ministries in such a way that they become hospitable and engaging entry points to your faith community?

   Mission and Social Activism Ministries?

   Small-Group Ministries?

   Preschool and After-School Ministries?

   Age-Level Ministries?

   Affinity Groups?

   Web, Social Media, and Digital Engagement?

Sixth Commandment

Thou Shall Watch the Throne: Rethink Leadership

Your day will come! Wait your turn! The idea is that the mantle of leadership has to be passed along in a certain way. Until it is your turn to lead, please go sit quietly, and we will call you at the appropriate time. Until it is your turn, "Watch the throne!" How long will those in the post-civil rights generations have to watch the throne? Is it when all those who came before are no longer around or physically able to lead? Is it when all those who came before are tired and ready to rest? Is it when all those who came before realize there is no one left to lead? We hope the answer is none of the above, but that is exactly where many congregations are headed if they are not careful.

What is the basis for leadership? In chapter one in Numbers, Moses chooses leaders from every tribe to help with the census. When we get to chapter thirteen in Numbers, Moses chooses different leaders to go on the mission to Canaan. We are not told the age of those chosen for the different missions, so it is not possible to say with certainty one group is older and the other is younger. We can speak with certainty that the leaders did change from the chapter one list to the list in chapter thirteen where Joshua is included. Up to this point we are familiar with Joshua as Moses's assistant, but now he is named as the leader of the Ephraimites (Num 13: 8).

Certainly one can argue that Joshua was groomed for leadership, and one can even speculate if he waited his turn. It is also important to think about performance, particularly of those taking on leadership positions. This means being a leader is not just about assuming a title, but requires a willingness to point others toward a particular future. Joshua eventually helps to point the Israelites to a new future. The challenge for many congregations is buying into the person (like Joshua) pointing them to a particular future, especially if that individual is young. Having just discussed the need for various entry points into congregations, in this chapter we will discuss the importance of resiliency on the part of post-civil rights individuals as it pertains to leadership.

Fear

Joseph is the son of Jacob's (Israel's) old age and his favorite. Joseph and his younger brother, Benjamin, are also the sons of Jacob's love and favorite wife, Rachel. As a younger son, Joseph should fall under the authority of his older brothers. This is why it is so troubling in Genesis 37:5-10 when Joseph shares his dreams with his family. The first dream (Gen 37:5-7) he shares with his brothers is about his sheaf rising up and their sheaves bowing down to him. The second dream he shares (Gen 37:9) with his brothers and father is about the sun, moon, and stars bowing to him. It should come as no surprise that his family does not appreciate his dreams. In fact, his father who adores Joseph (Gen 37:10-11), rebukes him for imaging such a thing as rising above his elders.

Let's bring this story closer to home so that it fits into our context. Imagine a twenty-something pastor at her first church assignment having a meeting with the decision-makers in the congregation. The pastor, in no uncertain terms, tells the decision-makers that they are to follow her into a new ministry in the city. The decision-makers all look at her with a smirk, because they are wondering who is this uninformed "child" thinking that she has a say in church business? The pastor is persistent and in the next few meetings repeats the same thing. Finally, one of the elders tells the pastor that she is wasting her breath.

There are countless ways of retelling what Joseph experiences when he shares his dreams with his family. Many of us in congregations love the Joseph narrative and even talk about how shortsighted Joseph's family was. We never realize our own fears and reservations are similar to Joseph's family as we continue to play out the Joseph narrative in our congregations. We treat younger individuals with dreams of doing something big just like Joseph's family treated him.

The backdrop to the Joseph narrative is his family perceives him as trying to usurp authority that is not his. Joseph is not the eldest son, and it is the eldest who should assume the title of authority. From the perspective of those in Joseph's family, it feels like Joseph is disrespecting them by trying to alter the lines of authority. The family does not really hear what Joseph says at a certain level because what strikes them is he thinks he should be over them. How dare someone his age think he should be in authority!

Joseph's family was operating with a particular understanding of authority that had been in place for years. The one in charge assumes the title, but it had nothing to do with gifts for leadership. The fact that Joseph's dreams turned this system upside down did not sit well with his family. The truth is, when someone like Joseph is in our midst, it often does not sit well with us either. We fear the unknown! We prefer the familiar even if it means going down a path that leads nowhere. What is fascinating is that the steps we will take may end up a bit like Joseph's brothers' efforts to protect the current system.

As you continue reading Genesis 37, Joseph's brothers are upset and decide to do something about it. They sell Joseph to the Ishmaelites to get him out of their hair. They feel good about this decision because their first inclination was to kill him. By getting rid of Joseph they feel they can set the system straight and those who are entitled to the throne (being in authority) will claim it. What they do not understand is God's mission is resilient and cannot be sold down the river.

When younger adults among us have dreams that would take us in a very different direction, do we not at times sell them down the river? We do not literally sell them into slavery, but we make comments or take actions to make sure they have no influence. We may not literally sell them down the river, but we do things like holding the key decision-making meetings at times when they are not available. By doing these things we feel we can keep the current system in place and thwart any attempts by those trying to change it. This is exactly what Joseph's brothers were doing in selling him into slavery.

What is the fear? One of the major fears is the system we bought into is going to change and we will no longer have a place (or as good a place) in the new system. This is one of the reasons why so many individuals dislike change. They feel like they have devoted themselves to a particular system and have staked their very essence on it. To have someone come along and change the playing field, especially if that person is younger, is way too much. This is the tension Joseph experienced and it is the one many post-civil rights individuals experience today in congregations.

Reality Check

If the Joseph story ended at the point of him being sold into slavery, then it would not give us much hope for systems changing. What the story does point out is both the challenge and reality facing congregations today. The reality is that when post-civil rights individuals are rejected and sold down the river, these individuals still flourish in a different setting and it is the church that is the worse for it. Joseph will eventually flourish in Egypt and until he steps in and helps, it is his family that suffers as a result of selling him into slavery.

The challenge is not to sell post-civil rights individuals down the river. We will never know what may have happened if Joseph was not sold. What we do know is that God still used that incident as a means of promoting Joseph and eventually helping his family. I will come back to this point later because it is key to congregations seeing hospitality to younger individuals in a different manner. I will focus for a moment on how Joseph engaged the opportunities for leadership that came his way.

Many in congregations think that the post-civil rights generations need us more than we need them. They have to fit into our system. The reality is when we sell this generation down the river, they are able to adapt because they are not beholden to the system. In Genesis 39:2, it says the "Lord was with Joseph so that he prospered." The phrase, "the Lord was with Joseph" should not be taken lightly. It gets at the heart of a leadership misconception: somehow God is only with those currently on the throne.

Once Joseph is sold into slavery in Egypt, it is easy to assume that his life is basically over and that he cannot prosper. The odds seem to be against Joseph. We make similar assumptions in congregations when it comes to post-civil rights individuals. We assume they cannot prosper or become leaders without the church. The Joseph text reminds us that "the Lord is with them" and they can prosper no matter where they go. God is not limited to a building or a particular system. When we ignore the insights and dreams of the post-civil rights generation we fall into the trap of thinking God is not with them.

God often works in unconventional ways. It is not hard to find in any city those in the post-civil rights generation doing their own thing. One example is a young pastor who is doing a new church start in Miami. The pastor is starting with small groups that are focused on a particular issue confronting people in the community. These various affinity groups get together once a month for worship. A part of the attraction for individuals who would never set foot in a traditional church is the leadership is diverse and encourages input from all generations. While this model may not work in a traditional setting, God is with this pastor and his team in their efforts.

What is interesting about the Joseph story is when we read the beginning of chapter 39 (God is with Joseph) we think things have turned and it will be smooth sailing for Joseph. But it is not smooth sailing for Joseph even though God is with him. The truth is Joseph has to learn to be resilient as he confronts the various challenges that come his way. Joseph is falsely accused by Potiphar's wife and lands in jail. It would be easy for Joseph to get discouraged and to give up at this point. What hopes can he have for prospering since he is in an Egyptian jail?

Think about the challenge many post-civil rights individuals face in trying to be leaders. Like Joseph, at times, they are accused of not going along with the plan. For example, a young pastor was on staff at a church that wanted to reach out to the post-civil rights generations. The young pastor was charged with making it happen. The pastor was successful, and people started coming to church. One day the senior pastor dropped by the associate's office and told him some of the longtime members had started complaining to him that the young pastor was ruining the church. The associate was confused and asked what was meant by the comment. The senior pastor shared their response that "all these new folk are taking our parking spots and sitting in our seats. They should know better!" The young pastor had done exactly what they wanted, but was still accused of ruining the church.

The need for resiliency is critical to survive the onslaught of challenges that will come when the post-civil rights generation seeks to be in leadership. Like Joseph, they will have to maintain hope when falsely accused of doing this or that. One of the ways Joseph was able to stay resilient is he continued to listen for God's voice. Joseph, relying on God, interprets the dreams of the cupbearer and the baker. It was two years later (really resilient) that Joseph gets an opportunity to interpret Pharaoh's dreams and get out of prison (Gen 41:1). If Joseph had given up, then he may never have had the opportunity to interpret Pharaoh's dreams.

The post-civil rights generation has to be resilient, because those on the throne will never move as quickly or buy-in as fully as those in the generation would like. The cupbearer in the Joseph text is a part of the royal system, but has done something to upset Pharaoh. Joseph brings the cupbearer good news, but when the cupbearer is restored he forgets about Joseph for two years. We do something similar in the church. We have wonderful children and youth programs to try and develop future leaders, but when the youth get to a point of wanting a "real say," all of a sudden they have no access to the throne. It is during these times that they must stay resilient like Joseph.

The last leadership quality I will lift up from the Joseph narrative is a willingness to take risks. Joseph demonstrates this characteristic throughout the narrative. He is willing to share his dreams with his family perhaps not realizing the danger of doing so. Joseph is not pulled in by Potiphar's wife, even though it may cost him his position (it does). Joseph interprets the dreams of the baker and cupbearer realizing the danger of being wrong. The key is Joseph is willing to take risks.

The risks Joseph takes are not about thrill seeking, but are grounded in an understanding of God's guidance in every situation. For example, the sharing of the dreams with his family are not about seeking to upset them and to bring harm upon himself, but it is about sharing the vision God gave to him. It is distinguishing between doing what we want and following God's lead that makes the difference in terms of risks. When we do what we want, it does not mean it will automatically fail, but it does mean we are not discerning where God is leading us. A building or stewardship campaign for a new worship center may be our vision for the congregation, but it may not be where God is really leading us. We may successfully build the new worship center, but the congregation also may be saddled with debt for the next twenty years, unable to do mission-oriented ministry.

One of the things that makes Joseph unique is his ability to continually discern God's will, so that the risks he is taking are not about his own agenda. This task is even more challenging for many in the post-civil rights generations who believe they have discerned God's vision appropriately and keep confronting roadblocks. This is why resiliency is so important, because those in the post-civil rights generation cannot give up the vision if it comes from God. The elapse of time between Joseph's original dream shared with his family and the fruition of it coming to be is years. Not getting discouraged between times is critical.

Taking risks definitely seems not safe for the church! The church, in the universal sense, is this entity built on a long tradition that seems adverse to risk. It is precisely because the church was willing to follow God's vision and take risks that it celebrates such a long tradition. Risk taking is about following God where others see no possibilities, but God has shown possibilities exist. It is easier to stay in our comfort zones and not put ourselves out there because we fear what may go wrong. More of us need to think like Joseph and be prepared for what is going to go right when following God's lead. This is what taking risk is all about!

Earlier in this chapter, I stated that we never will know how the vision God gave Joseph would have come to fruition if his brothers had not sold him into slavery. We do know that God used what did happen to Joseph to still bring about transformation. In fact, in Genesis 50:20, Joseph tells his brothers, "You intended to harm me, but God intended it for good to accomplish what is now being done, the saving of many lives." This quote by Joseph speaks to all of the generations in the church. God's vision is larger than any of us can imagine and will come to fruition even when we attempt to thwart it.

Selling the post-civil rights generations down the river will not stop them from assuming leadership positions and following God's vision. It just means that God will find another way to use these individuals to bring about the vision. This is what happened with Joseph and it continues to happen today. The Rev. Telley Lynnette Gadson is an example of someone from the post-civil rights generations who followed God's vision at St. Mark's United Methodist Church in Sumter, South Carolina, and helped them revitalize physically and spiritually.[1] Rev. Gadson worked with the congregation and empowered them with tools of stewardship to raise the necessary funds to do the building project when it seemed like things had stalled. It was not always easy for her, but she was committed to following God's vision and God's vision came to fruition in ways even she could not imagine.

Generational competition has always been around and will always be around. The reality is that God has always used those in younger generations to carry out God's mission. The story of Joseph is just one biblical reminder of the younger generation being placed in a position of leadership. If we are truly following a biblical model, then we should be open to those from younger generations assuming positions of leadership and not discouraging them.

Thou Shall Watch the Throne

The sixth commandment is Thou Shall Watch the Throne. A throne denotes leadership. In too many of our congregations we have preconceived ideas of who should and should not be in leadership. What is amazing is, even given all of our human meddling, God still finds a way to move forward God's mission. God's mission is resilient! The insight for all of us is God's mission is not based upon age; it is God who calls and empowers individuals to live out the mission at any given time. If we are focused on God's mission and not the throne, then we are opening ourselves to bringing it to fruition.

Covenant Practice: Resilient

1. Who in your church are leaders from the post-civil rights generations? What leadership roles do they have?

2. What fears might your church have about following a leader from the post-civil rights generations?

3. Think of an example where a post-civil rights person has been sold down the river. Are mechanisms in place in your congregation to sell post-civil rights individuals seeking leadership down the river? How can you dismantle these mechanisms?

4. How can your congregation use the Joseph text to prepare itself for a different leadership style (understanding God's mission is resilient)?

Seventh Commandment

Thou Shall Get Game: Engage Mission and Activism in Meaningful Ways

Got Game: When a person is very good at something—it doesn't even have to be a game, just anything they're good at[1]

One could describe Caleb as one who "got game"! "The LORD spoke to Moses: Send out men to explore the land of Canaan, which I'm giving to the Israelites. Send one man from each ancestral tribe, each a chief among them. So Moses sent them out from the Paran desert according to the LORD's command. All the men were leaders among the Israelites."[2] Caleb was among the identified leadership of Israel. In Numbers 13:6, Caleb is identified as the representative to the delegation "from the tribe of Judah, Caleb son of Jephunneh." Caleb did not sign up for this assignment; rather, he was appointed to this assignment. When Caleb returned from his assignment, he returned with answers to the questions that were asked of him. Yet, Caleb's data, which was identical to the data that the other leaders gathered, yielded a very different conclusion than the majority of the delegation. The majority of the delegation returned to Moses and the Israelite people afraid, discouraged, and defeated. Can you imagine what they were thinking? Maybe they thought: Why would God promise us something that is not possible for us to obtain? Yet, while they reported all the reasons why they could not go on to the land of Canaan as God promised; Caleb brought a minority report—"'We must go up and take possession of it, because we are more than able to do it.'"[3] Again we are not proposing hegemony by overcoming others, but the emphasis on going is critical. In this chapter we discuss the importance of congregations answering the call to go.

The Failure of Nerve to GO

When it comes to engaging in mission and social activism, many of our congregations suffer from what Edwin H. Friedman called, "a failure of nerve."[4] In light of the failure of nerve that many congregational leaders face, Friedman challenges leaders who are "highly anxious risk-avoiders" and more concerned with people pleasing and feeling good than with making progress to take risks. These leaders do not like to cause ripples or ruffle feathers. Rather, they work hard to keep people happy and comfortable. Like the majority in Caleb's delegation, they size up the land and declare what cannot be done. Instead of trusting the direction of God to move forward to new places, they allow fear to prevent missional engagement. Congregational leadership that strives for the comfort of the people in the pews—often in the name of positive income statements—rarely challenge the people to faithful living. And as Jesus reminds us, one of the marks of faithful and fruitful living for the Christian disciples is engaging in mission and social activism.

In commissioning the twelve disciples, Jesus admonished them to "go instead to the lost sheep, the people of Israel. As you go, make this announcement: 'The kingdom of heaven has come near.' Heal the sick, raise the dead, cleanse those with skin diseases, and throw out demons. You received without having to pay. Therefore, give without demanding payment."[5] And after Jesus was raised from the dead, Jesus asked Simon Peter three times, "do you love me more than these?" And three times Peter answered, "Yes, LORD; you know I love you." Then Jesus responded and instructed, "Feed my lambs.... Take care of my sheep.... Feed my sheep.... [and even when you are led where you do not want to go] Follow me."[6] Even still, congregations are hesitant to move beyond their pews and outside of the walls of their buildings in the name of fear of unfamiliar people and places. Congregations are hesitant to take a risk for what they do not know and they are unwilling to give up their perceived comfort.

Ignoring the Call

In the United States, the culture is transient and mobile. A large majority of people spend immense amounts of time in their vehicles in transit from one place to another. Congregations drive in and out of communities to go to places that they are familiar with or have a connection to, without concern or acknowledgment for the people that they pass as they travel along. We pass the very people to whom God has sent us, all the while failing to see them and to heed the call of Jesus to go, heal, raise, cleanse, throw out, love, tend, feed, and transform. Some communities that we pass through are rich in tangible resources and other communities are rich in heritage and population resources. Some communities are rolling with green grass and picket fences and other communities are fortified in bars and gates. Some communities are home to people who look and sound like us; while other communities are home to people who terrify us—perhaps because we have no frame of reference for communication or relationship with them. Yet, because we are all created in and by the love of God, as people of sacred worth, these are all communities to be considered flowing with milk and honey. They are all worth something. They are all places to which we are sent. Yet, we cannot go because we are paralyzed by our preoccupation with our stuff and our lives, by our selfishness, and by our fear.

All these years after God sent Caleb and the leader-spies and all these years after Jesus sent the twelve, God is still calling and sending congregations to their Canaan. We must take care to understand that God is not calling us to conquer people; rather, God is calling us to partner with people in Christ's transformative mission in the world. Yet, the challenge still lies ahead of us: if congregations are going to do the work that God has called them to, they cannot do it from their pews, pulpits, fellowship halls, Sunday school rooms, computers, and smart devices. Congregations must GO!

In Deuteronomy 1, God reminds the Israelites of the call God gave them in Numbers 13. The Israelites have ignored that God told them to "go." God rebukes them for not following through on what God told them and for not believing what God promised them. They were so busy being afraid and playing it safe that they failed to recognize the gift that God was giving them in a new place. In Deuteronomy 1:26-33, the Lord reminds them:

> But you were unwilling to go up; you rebelled against the command of the LORD your God. You grumbled in your tents and said, "The LORD hates us; so he brought us out of Egypt to deliver us into the hands of the Amorites to destroy us. Where can we go? Our brothers have made our hearts melt in fear. They say, 'The people are stronger and taller than we are; the cities are large, with walls up to the sky. We even saw the Anakites there.'" Then I said to you "Do not be terrified; do not be afraid of them. The LORD your God, who is going before you, will fight for you, as he did for you in Egypt, before your very eyes, and in the wilderness. There you saw how the LORD your God carried you, as a father carries his son, all the way you went until you reached this place." In spite of this, you did not trust in the LORD your God, who went ahead of you on your journey, in fire by night and in a cloud by day, to search out places for you to camp and to show you the way you should go.

Where is God calling you to go? To whom is God calling your congregation? Why are you not going? Do not be afraid.

Preparation for the Journey

When preparing congregations to engage in mission and social activism, congregational leaders often make the mistake of sending unprepared congregants to pick the places and issues in which the rest of the congregation will engage. When God sent the Israelites to Canaan, God was very specific about the qualifying credentials of those who would go on the fact-finding mission. God told Moses to send the leaders. These leaders would have been prepared for the journey. These would not have been your run-of-the-mill pew members; rather, they would have been tried-and-true disciples. These leaders were so invested in the mission that their names and lineages are recorded in Numbers 13:4-16. They were people who grew up with and possessed a mature faith in God. These leaders were proven and would have studied to show themselves approved. They believed in following God and God's messenger, Moses. They were already taking responsibility for the well-being of the Israelites.

In today's society, we would consider these leaders the people whose names are on the cornerstone of the church building, on the sides of the pews, on plaques in the fellowship hall, and on the chartering documents of the congregation. These are the committed Sunday school teachers who model mature discipleship to others. This is the top tier—it does not get any better! Moses couldn't have picked anybody better than these twelve to understand the mission. Congregational leaders: do not send the unprepared to lead the congregation into new missional and social engagement; the mission is hard enough for those who have the training, let alone those who don't. Even though the leaders were sent to scope out Canaan, only Caleb and Joshua came back with a favorable report that matched the word of the Lord (Num 14:6-9). The lesson in this is that even when you send your best and brightest to lead the congregation into new ways of engaging in mission and social activism, they may not understand or get onboard. Even still, it only takes one to see and run with the vision that is laid out before them. Of all the talented, prepared, and disciplined leadership that was sent to Canaan, only Caleb and Joshua could see what God saw—an invitational opportunity for expansion.

Congregational leaders must invest time in preparing congregations—both leaders and followers—for understanding new ways of mission and social activism. Children learn to ride bikes on training wheels. Teachers learn to teach with clinical and practical hours supervised by seasoned teachers. Disciples learn to serve at the feet of master servants. In heeding the congregational call to engage in mission and social activism, congregational leaders must be willing to train the people and provide healthy models of missional engagement before sending them out.

Many congregations view mission as serving people who are in a lower economic status or a less fortunate life situation than they. They view missional engagement as helping to alleviate a problem that others have—generally, poverty. In the book, *When Helping Hurts: How To Alleviate Poverty Without Hurting The Poor And Yourself,*[7] Steve Corbett and Brian Fikkert outline a variety of missional approaches that hinder and hurt the people God sends us to serve. In pointing out that every human being is broken in some way, they warn us that if we are unwilling to acknowledge our "mutual brokenness," we set ourselves up to do more harm than good in our mission work. Corbett and Fikkert challenge the economically rich to an awareness of a "god-complex" that results in an intentional or unintentional superiority complex. They challenge the church to remember and practice that when we serve in mission, we are all the same and we all seek reconciliation and restoration with God and each other. Corbett and Fikkert challenge congregations, when engaging in ministry with the poor, to "discern whether the situation calls for relief, rehabilitation, or development. The failure to distinguish among these situations is one of the most common reasons that poverty-alleviation efforts often do harm." Engaging in meaningful mission is not done to or for people, but with people.

Leaders are admonished to help congregations gain an understanding that in Christian mission, congregants are tasked to build people up and not tear them down. We are not to do things for people that they can do for themselves. In doing so, we render them helpless. Meaningful missional engagement is about building relationships and primarily the redemptive relationship that we have in Christ Jesus. We are not the savior; Christ is the Savior of the world. Congregations are called and sent in mission **WITH**—not mission to or mission for!

New Places of Mission and Social Activism

Where are the new places of mission and social activism to which God is calling your congregation? This is a question that is only answered with deep discernment and by following the lead of the Holy Spirit. While I was serving as an associate pastor in a congregation located in downtown Atlanta, Georgia, the clergy and lay leadership of the congregation decided that after decades of experiencing decline and turning inward, it was time to do something different in order to reverse the trend of decline. They spent a great deal of time, energy, and resources discerning the will of God for their next steps. One of the places God led the congregation was into a churchwide engagement in mission, specifically, local mission. The expectation was communicated that every member would be invited to find a place of missional service through the congregation. This congregation ascertained its community's greatest needs and formed partnerships with several local organizations that were engaging in impactful missional work. Not only was the city better served by an increase in people and financial resources, but the congregation was strengthened in discipleship and in number because of the missional and social engagement that they took on. This was not an easy journey. Naysayers and nonsupporters voiced their opposition. Every original mission partnership did not stick. Even still, God honored the efforts of the congregation because they were obedient and faithful to the call of their congregational lives.

An unintended consequence of this commitment to social activism and missional engagement was that it attracted young adults who were moving into the community. Missional engagement became the primary entry point to the congregation, changed the reputation of the congregation in the community, and increased its visibility and viability as a transformational ministry in the community. A church battling the debilitating blows of decades of decline began to experience exponential growth that was intergenerational, multicultural, multiethnic from the spectrum of socioeconomic backgrounds. When asked why they came to the church, one person remarked, "You people actually act like Christians. You mean what you say and you say what you mean. You are doing the work of God!" God's admonition to engage in mission and social activism is hard and sacred work. It is beyond us and in spite of us. Yet, when God sends, we should go. If God sends, then you will certainly be equipped for the journey ahead!

New places of mission and social activism may look like the local school or the community soccer and football fields. They may be the work cubicles and even the Sunday school class that functions more as a breeding ground for gossip and cliques than a training ground for disciples. But new places of mission and social activism are also to be found deep in the barrio or the ghetto. They are to be found at the courthouse and the state house advocating for children, education, prison reform, the eradication of the death penalty, and other policies. They may be on graffiti-covered basketball courts that have no nets and are riddled with bullet holes. It may be the housing projects that smell and on street corners where you can smell the drugs. It might be in a prison. It might be at a homeless shelter. It might be right outside the door of your church and you've missed it because you've been busy maintaining brick, mortar, and popularity. This is the work of God's people. This is the task of the congregation.

Congregations who engage in new ways of mission and social activism must first understand that this will change your church and your congregants. It will disturb the status quo in such a way that the faithful may not understand or approve. Just as a majority of the leaders that returned from Canaan refused to move forward, many of the disciples in your church may be unsettled by the change that missional and social engagement brings about. People will come to the church looking for the people who were bold enough to engage them on their turf and on their terms. They may come looking for the "church people" who were courageous enough to move out of their pews and into the streets. They may sit in previously reserved pews and want to be a part of ministries previously open only to a select few. They may irritate the status quo and upset the powers that be.

Congregational leaders may have to move slowly into seasons of uncomfortable and challenging missional and social engagement. Yet, still holding congregants accountable to the holy tension of the countercultural sending gospel and the task of congregational nurture. United Methodist scholar Dr. Thomas E. Frank put it this way, "Congregations help people to find their place, encourage them to make a place, and comfort them when they do not fit a place...giving people solace and language for sustaining individual and family vitality in a social milieu of constant striving."[8] Once we help people find their place, we must push them out of the nest to help others find their place.

Engaging the Post-Civil Rights Generations

If the church is to engage post-civil rights generations, congregations must do the hard work of understanding new ways of engaging in mission and social activism. Pushing through to this understanding is to be done before engaging post-civil rights generations. Congregations cannot air their dirty laundry of disagreement on these issues if they are to engage post-civil rights generations. Congregations must learn to agree to disagree in holy ways in places of social activism when they do not agree. We must model loving through disagreement. And when we do, we must provide spaces and opportunities through which to live out the mandate to be the hands and feet of Christ in our communities and throughout the world. After all, the Lord says over and over again, "Do not be terrified. Just go."

The church can stand the reminder that post-civil rights generations have proven their commitment to service and the pursuit of meaning through their vast commitment to the nonprofit sector and to national movements to raise money and serve in places that seem unlikely. "Mission ministries" like Teach For America and the Peace Corps and a growing trend to take a year off between high school and college or after college to travel and serve prove this. Peter Gomes named the impressive "moral curiosity" of the post-civil rights generations and "their desire to know, to be, and to do good."[9] These are the same generations that have been tagged as selfish, self-centered, and godless; yet, they are seeking meaning and a place to belong. If the church will understand and engage in mission and social activism, the church can provide a place for these generations to live out their passion to matter. This is the work of transformation. This is the mission of the church—to go, make, and transform.

Thou Shall Get Game

The seventh commandment is Thou Shall Get Game. When it comes to missional and social engagement, the post-civil rights generations are ahead of the church because they "got game" when it comes to serving others. They are often fearless when it comes to going to new places and trying new things. By and large, in spite of their perceived entitlement complexes, many understand what it means to serve and what it means to be a servant. And the people to whom God is sending the church cannot wait any longer for churches to decide that everyone is on board with engaging in mission and social engagement. How do you suppose the land of Canaan became a land of milk and honey in the first place? Somebody had to go there, uproot, plant, tear down, build up, and transform. We do not go in the name of mission and social activism to take over. We do not even go to do it our way. We do not engage in mission to prove our goodness. We engage in mission and social activism to be in ministry with God's people on God's behalf. "Trust in the LORD your God, who went ahead of you on your journey, in fire by night and in a cloud by day, to search out places for you... and to show you the way you should go" (Deut 1:32-33). If the truth be told, then your places of missional engagement are your congregation's ticket out of the wilderness. Jeremiah 29 reminds us, your welfare is tied up in the welfare of the place to which I've sent you, says the Lord. Dear church, your welfare is tied up in understanding meaningful ways of engaging in mission and social engagement.

Covenant Practice: Going

1. Currently how is your church involved in mission and social activism? What are the needs of your community? If you don't know, suggest ways to find out.

2. Has your congregation experienced a failure of nerve when it comes to engaging in mission and social activism? In what ways?

3. Discuss how to create a congregational discernment process where you can listen to God's call. Where are the new places of mission and social activism to which God is calling your congregation? To whom is God calling you? What's the best way to answer God's call?

4. If you have post-civil rights generations in your church,

what do they say about their own mission and social activism?

5. Write down some ways your church can better engage post-civil rights generations in missions and social activism? Share your ideas with your pastor and other church leaders.

Eighth Commandment

Thou Shall Not Deny My Swag: Hear New Insights

I-majored-in-swagger-swag-swoop-swoop-swoop-swoop-swagger-swag-swoop-swag-swoop-swag[1]

— *"The Swag Song" by JusReign*

Swag has become an everyday word that speaks to how someone carries himself or herself. For example, someone who is stylish, confident, and catches everyone's eye is often characterized as having swag. A biblical way of understanding swag is looking at the actions of Caleb. In Numbers 13:40, after the majority spy report, Caleb tells all of Israel that they can go into the promised land. Talk about swag! The majority of the spies are scared, and Caleb is full of confidence. Caleb carries himself differently than the majority of the spies.

What is it that gives Caleb his swag? In this chapter, we will seek to understand swag from a particular biblical perspective that challenges mature generations to take note of those in post-civil rights generations. Congregations cannot be scared of moving forward in a different direction, but need to carry themselves with a certain swagger. This is not an egotistical swagger, but one shaped by an encounter with God. This chapter is about not misunderstanding those in the post-civil rights generation so that we can truly hear them.

Don't Be Sca*rrr*ed

A struggling congregation that needed new life decided to enter into an agreement with a congregation that was seeking a building for worship. The congregation seeking the building was different ethnically from the current congregation and also much younger. The hope was for the two congregations to be able to do some things together that could lead to new life permeating the building.

After about a month the congregation who was allowing the congregation to rent worship space started complaining to the pastor. They started telling the pastor about how the new congregation moved the microphones, left the drums up on the side of the sanctuary (a few who attended one of the worship services complained the drums were too loud), and folk they did not know were coming into the building. The pastor replied, "Is this not what we were hoping, that new life would come into the building?" Those complaining did not see it as new life, but as a precursor to something worse to come.

The pastor understood that the microphones being moved and the drums being left were irritating, but the real issue was new individuals who they did not know coming into the building. They were afraid of folk stealing things from the building. They wanted the pastor to put a stop to the new folk coming in because they were scared of what might happen. It was okay for those who rented the space to come, but no one else should show up. Eventually the visiting congregation stopped renting space and things went back to "normal."

I hope you are struck by the line, "They were scared by what might happen." How many congregations are scared by what might happen? Congregations are more comfortable with things being normal, which often means nothing happening. These congregations are often comfortable with decline and not seeking new possibilities because they are scared. The example of the congregation in the story above illustrates this point. Some may be thinking maybe they have a reason for being scared and we should not make light of it. Certainly we are not intending to make light of criminal activity (their worry about stealing). We are, however, suggesting that simply attending a worship service should not qualify as criminal activity.

The fact is the new individuals coming should have been perceived as a blessing and not as a source of worry. The congregation renting the space wanted that particular space, because they were confident that they could reach new folk in the area. They were not scared of those in the area. The congregation renting had a swagger about them for how to engage in ministry that the current congregation did not. Fear can paralyze a whole community and keep them from moving forward as we learned in the story above and as we will learn in the Israelites' encounter with Goliath.

David is a biblical character who has swag. In the story of David and Goliath the Israelites are afraid of facing Goliath. It is David who has the swagger to face Goliath when no one else will go up against him. In 1 Samuel 17:1-50, we read about David's defeat of Goliath. Our focus is not so much on David defeating Goliath as it is on David being young and having a certain swag that was threatening to others. Two individuals threatened by David's swag in different ways are his eldest brother, Eliab, and Goliath.

We are told in 1 Samuel 17:28 that Eliab is the eldest brother of eight and that David is the youngest. We do not know the age difference between them, but it is reasonable that Eliab could represent more mature generations and David, post-civil rights generations. David is sent by his father to take rations to his brothers at the camp, but David gets caught up in the drama of Goliath the Philistine challenging the Israelites (1 Sam 17:20-24). David overhears that King Saul will greatly reward anyone willing to face Goliath. No one has been willing to face Goliath for forty days because all of the Israelites fear him (1 Sam 17:24). They were scared!

David started asking different people what would happen if someone stepped up to the plate and faced Goliath. They kept telling David the king would reward that person greatly (1 Sam 17:25-27)! Eliab overhears David asking questions and states in 1 Samuel 17:28, "Why have you come down here? And with whom did you leave those few sheep in the wilderness? I know how conceited you are and how wicked your heart is; you came down only to watch the battle." Eliab is telling David to stay out of affairs that are not his own. Eliab believes David should concern himself with watching the sheep because that is the job of a young lad. What Eliab is not saying out loud is, fighting is a "man's" job. Of course Eliab, like the others, is too scared to face Goliath and has not gone forward to meet his challenge.

David, unlike his brother, goes to Saul and agrees to face Goliath (1 Sam 17:32). What Eliab called conceit was a part of David's swag. David was not scared like the others to face Goliath because, as he reports in 1 Samuel 17:34-37, he has already faced lions and bears. In verse 37, David states that God was with him and David is confident that God will be with him now. David may be young, but he carries himself in a certain way because he believes all things are possible through God.

How many times are we like Eliab—talking down to younger folk and telling them to stay out of affairs that do not pertain to them? The reality is, the affairs do pertain to them because they impact their future just like they do our future. If no one faces Goliath and the Israelites are subjects of the Philistines, then this impacts David's future. The argument that young folk should stay out of affairs that do not pertain to them is nonsensical in many instances, because they are just as impacted as others by decisions. The way the church moves forward in participating in God's reign impacts everyone regardless of age.

Eliab also was threatened by David's presence at the camp because he figured David should attend to his job of keeping sheep—stay in his place. David kept asking different individuals what would happen if someone faced Goliath and his brother Eliab perceived this as unnecessary interference. Eliab tells David in so many words, "You have the responsibility of taking care of the sheep—stay quiet and do it." Congregations often mirror Eliab by telling post-civil rights generations, "Concern yourself with youth activities and leave the real issues to us."

The bottom line is these congregations are stating that we do not want to hear from you unless it is about your area. Why are we afraid of hearing the voices of younger generations? Are we scared like Eliab that they have the swag to face those things that scare us? Most often the reason given for not listening to younger generations is they have not experienced all that older generations have experienced. This is a way of saying they do not know as much as us and therefore should not have a say. Certainly this observation is true, but we never lift up the flip side of the coin to this point. Because the younger generations have not experienced as much as mature generations, they are more willing to try new things without worrying about past failures. The famous phrase, "We tried it before," keeps many congregations from moving forward. If one does not have those experiences, then trying something new is easier. While experience is important, we need to consider both sides of the coin and not just one side.

After David's encounter with his brother, David steps up to the plate and agrees to face Goliath (1 Sam 17:32). What is interesting about this part of the text is Saul dresses David in his tunic to go into battle (1 Sam 17:38). It is analogous to the mature generations dressing-up the ideas of post-civil rights generations to move the church forward. Doug Powe addresses this issue when suggesting some individuals within mature generations are "hoping that the post-civil rights generations will become the mirror image of their generations…"[2] The result is facing the challenges before us with the same outlook as previous generations.

When David put on Saul's tunic and the rest of his gear, he quickly realized it was not comfortable. It did not fit and weighed him down (1 Sam 17:38-39). Many in the post-civil rights generations understand that they cannot simply be like past generations because it weighs them down. This in no way suggests ignoring the insights from past generations, but it does mean allowing more current generations to face the challenges in their own way. Saul, by putting his tunic on David, was still trying to dictate the way in which David should move forward. Saul was not allowing room for God to act creatively through David.

David Kinnaman writes, "As Christians, we want to believe our efforts are driven by the right motivations. We assume we are pursuing God and his purposes."[3] Kinnaman is working with Isaiah 58, but his words are applicable to what we are suggesting is taking place in this 1 Samuel 17 passage. Saul believed his motives were right in trying to put David in his tunic. Many in mature generations believe their motives are right in trying to dictate to post-civil rights generations. The truth is as Kinnaman points out; we often have the wrong motivations. This is not done on purpose, but the result can still be disastrous. We need to let those in post-civil rights generations move forward in a way that is comfortable for them. We need to listen to them and not dictate to them. David realizes this and takes off Saul's tunic and gear because it did not really fit.

Interestingly, it is because David does not appear like a typical warrior that Goliath notices his swag. He notices it because it's not the normal or usual course of events. Goliath is used to fighting individuals dressed in a certain way when they come out for battle. David challenges this norm and it catches Goliath off guard to the point that Goliath does not take David seriously.

In 1 Samuel 17:43, Goliath says to David, "'Am I a dog, that you come at me with sticks?' And the Philistine cursed David by his gods." Goliath was expecting someone dressed like him ready for battle to come and face him, not some youngster with sticks. Goliath is insulted that David would think he could challenge him. Goliath's anger is expressed in verse 44 where he threatens to give David's carcass to the "birds and wild animals." Many of us do not want to admit it, but Goliath's attitude is often ours toward those in post-civil rights generations. We are insulted when they confront challenges with new ideas or new insights. We do not want to listen!

For example, we know about a congregation that faced a space dilemma because it did not have a nursery. The good news was the congregation was experiencing growth in families with young children. The challenge was they did not have any space for the children to learn and grow. A couple of the newer mothers suggested switching space with a Sunday school class that had existed for twenty-five years and had dwindled to seven people. This particular Sunday school class had the largest classroom space, even though the actual attendance to class was small. The newer moms figured since the class had dwindled down, they did not need all that space.

You would have thought the moms told the class they were repossessing all of their belongings. The class would not hear of giving up a space they had owned for twenty-five years. Like Goliath, the class was insulted by a paradigm shift that moved away from the norm. In the mind of those who were a part of the class, another solution that did not require them shifting their worldview needed to be found. While we all like to think of ourselves as the underdog like David, the reality is we are often like Goliath threatened by something that is outside of our norm.

To make matters worse, David has the swag to stand up to Goliath in the Lord's name. According to 1 Samuel 17:45-47, David responds to Goliath not about his own ability, but God's. David understood that it is God who is creatively at work doing new things and not us. David's swag is not based upon his own ability, but on his confidence in God to do what seems impossible. Certainly our understanding of swag differs from popular perceptions of swag on this point. Swag is not about us but about God. God works through us to do the impossible, but we should never be confident in our own abilities. David was not scared because he was confident in God.

This is the confidence that congregations need to gain. It is a confidence in God to act and do a new thing. God often uses younger generations as messengers to do a new thing. Congregations should be open to hearing post-civil rights generations and not be scared. We will outline what this means for congregations in the next section.

New Possibilities

An aging congregation with just a few young people, but some financial resources, decided to use all of its resources helping others before closing the church. The congregation decided to start sponsoring community meals for families one evening a week. The congregation figured in about a year it would use up its resources and close its doors. A funny thing happened on the way to closing. In a few months, the congregation noticed more intergenerational families coming to service than previously. The families coming to the meals had discovered the church.

The congregation rediscovered its missional purpose in the community, helping it to create a new swag. The new swag was not ego driven, based upon the congregation having resources and others in the community not having resources. The swag was driven by a willingness to let God use them to touch the lives of others in a genuine manner. They fully invested themselves in the meals and the community responded because they experienced something new at the congregation. For the first time in awhile, the community experienced a sense of welcoming that went beyond simply filling some pews. Those in the community at the meal felt like they were being heard. The congregation, when it thought it was closing, stopped worrying about filling the pews and started engaging individuals to form genuine relationships.

We all can learn something about new possibilities from the story above that can help us to appreciate the swag of post-civil rights generations. One take-away from the story is stop being inward focused and remember our missional calling. Many in the post-civil rights generations are interested in impacting the world. Congregations that are simply seeking to fill the pews are moving in the opposite direction. These congregations often deny the swag of post-civil rights generations because they want to get out and do new things. These congregations want individuals to come in and find them.

It was not until the congregation in the above story went out and sought those in the community that something different started happening. The church continued to decline as long as they stayed inward focused. Instead of squashing the dreams and visions of post-civil rights generations for doing new things, we should support these efforts. The prophet Joel said, "And afterward, I will pour out my Spirit on all people. Your sons and daughters will prophesy, your old men will dream dreams, your young men will see visions" (Joel 2:28). Joel is suggesting that all generations have a role in God's plan and not just older generations. Interestingly, Peter picks up this text from Joel in Acts 2:17 and following, when he addresses the crowd after the Holy Spirit descends.

From the beginning, the church was supposed to be intergenerational. When congregations turn inward and stop listening to those in the post-civil rights generations, they are ceasing to be the church where God's Spirit has been poured out on all people. In very practical language, this means paying attention to ideas that come from younger folk. It means a willingness to try new things that the church has not done before even if there is a possibility of failure. Most importantly, it means that the Holy Spirit is at work in all people and not just a few people.

Another take-away from the story at the beginning of this section is related to discipleship. Discipleship is about being genuine and not pretending to be something you are not. At first glance, this may seem contradictory to having swag. In fact, one can argue this is precisely why some seek to deny the swag of those in post-civil rights generations because they are pretending to be something that they are not. They are putting on airs! The key to our understanding of swag is it comes from God and not the person. David's success against Goliath was his emphasis on God and not his own skills. Others like his brother, Eliab, took this for cockiness, but David really just had a swag for God.

When the congregation, in the story at the beginning of this section, put away the pretensions of not trying to keep alive who they used to be and started genuinely engaging others in the community, things changed. The younger families started taking them seriously and engaging them. The dinners were not just another attempt to get individuals into the pew, but were a genuine act of hospitality. The members in the congregation simply wanted people to come eat and have a good time. This is the spirit in which they invited others to join them. This is the spirit in which we can have a swag in God.

God is not asking for copycat congregations. This means every congregation is not going to have 10,000, 5,000, or even 500 members. God is asking that every congregation live out its missional calling in a genuine manner as it engages others. Being genuine means a willingness to open one's self up to others in a manner that allows them to really see you. In Acts 2, prior to Peter reinterpreting the Joel text for the crowd that day, we are told each one was able to hear in their own language (Acts 2:6). When those in the crowd opened themselves up to the Spirit and put aside the barriers that typically separated them, they were able to hear in their own language!

Talk about really being able to hear someone for the first time. They were able to hear in a way that made sense to them individually, which allowed them to see things differently. So when Peter speaks with a swag starting in Acts 2:14, he does so, not based upon his own ego, but on God's actions. We are convinced that those in the post-civil rights generations are seeking genuine connections that point to God's actions. The question is, "Are we willing to participate with them in experiencing this gift from the Holy?" If we are, then it means there are always new possibilities for our congregations.

Thou Shall Not Deny My Swag

The eighth commandment is Thou Shall Not Deny My Swag. There are a lot of egotistical individuals in the world, but we should not confuse ego with swag for God. David had swag for God and this enabled him to challenge Goliath when others were scared. Congregations have to stop being scared of declining and move into the future knowing God will walk with them. If congregations are genuine in the way they represent God, then those in post-civil rights generations may walk into a new future with us. This also means congregations must recognize God has poured out the Spirit on all people and not just a few!

Covenant Practice: Listen

1. Who are people in your congregation who have swag for God?

2. Is the swag of younger generations different from that of older generations? Are you threatened by the swag of

younger generations? Name some ways that your congregation may have tried to squash things promoted by younger generations.

3. Have younger generations suggested new possibilities for your congregation? Did you listen? Name those ideas.

4. What steps can you take as a congregation to being more genuine in relationships with others?

5. Who are some people whom your congregation needs to listen to in your church, in your community, in your denomination?

Ninth Commandment

Thou Shall Sample: Bring Together the Old and New

Sampling is one of the ways that hip hop pays homage to those who paved the way, but also shifts the way we think about the original song. Two of the most sampled songs are "Atomic Dog" by George Clinton and "The Payback" by James Brown.[1] LL Cool J. used "The Payback" in his hit "Boomin System."[2] You can hear it playing in the background as LL spits his raps. When LL did "Boomin System," "The Payback" had already been around for about seventeen years. He took something that was older and used his genre to make it relevant for a new generation of individuals.

In Numbers 14, we have an example of sampling by the Israelites. Many of the Israelites "raised their voices . . . against Moses and Aaron." They complained about being brought out of Egypt and how things were better in Egypt (Num 14:1-3). In fact, in verse 4 it reads, "We should choose a leader and go back to Egypt." Many of the Israelites wanted to give up their freedom and go back into bondage! This is obviously an example of negative sampling.

By negative sampling I mean the Israelites are reaching back for something in their past, but it is not helpful. Lucy Jones, a blogger, writes a list of samples gone wrong and her point is the samples often do not help us to see something new—it is a bad mix.[3] The same is true of the Israelites in this instance in the way they are sampling from the past; it is a bad mix. They are longing for the glorious past, but the reality is the past was not that good. Sound familiar to some congregations?

There is also good sampling in the Numbers 14 text. By good sampling we mean trying to pull from the tradition in a way that the Israelites will see something new. This is what Joshua does in Numbers 14:6-9, but alas, even his attempt at good sampling fails in this instance because the majority still wants to stone him (Num 14:10). Joshua addresses the Israelites and basically tries to remind them that Yahweh has made a covenant to be with them (Num 14: 6-9). Joshua does not use the word *covenant* in his speech, but he does talk about not rebelling against God and that God would be with them. The covenant has two parts. One is that God promises to be their God and the people promise to worship only God. Joshua seeks to remind the assembly that even as they face new challenges, the covenant remains. Joshua was trying to make the covenant relevant to their current circumstances in exile by sampling from the past, but the majority of the Israelites were not having it. Many of our congregations are not much different today in the way that they sample from the past. At times they tend to forget those practices (e.g., community involvement) that made them vibrant and only pull from traditions that make moving forward more challenging. At other times, they create a mix that is more fruitful and moves the congregation forward in a new and exciting way. The goal is to create good mixes that move congregations forward toward inclusive messages.

The Master Sampler

When one reads the gospels closely it becomes evident that Jesus is the master sampler. Jesus pulls from what is old to try and help the Israelites to see something new. For example, in Luke 4:18-20, Jesus reads from the Isaiah scroll, and claims it as his ministry. The end of verse 20 reads, "the eyes of everyone in the synagogue were fastened on him." Jesus sampled from Isaiah making it clear that the future is bright because the prophecy has been fulfilled.

Are we saying that sampling is easy and someone must simply pick a Bible verse and read it in their congregation today? Not exactly! What makes Jesus's sampling so compelling is the way in which Jesus understands the audience. For example, in Luke 10:25-37, Jesus surprises the audience by pulling from the tradition (Lev 19:18) and helping them to understand who is our neighbor. The audience expected Jesus to say one of their own (Israelites) was going to be a neighbor, but Jesus helps them to see what it means to be a neighbor (Samaritans who were despised can be) in a new way by pulling from the tradition.

Inclusive Community

In Luke 2:41-48a, we learn that Jesus is left behind in the temple. The text is clear that Jesus is a boy (Luke 2: 43), but that he is respected by the teachers in the temple because there is mutual engagement (Luke 2:46). By mutual engagement I mean that Jesus asks them questions and listens to them. This give-and-take is important and a model for all congregations.

Obviously we cannot speak for every young person during Jesus's day, but here we have an example of Jesus engaged in a mutual exchange with the teachers in the temple. The fact that the teachers had no issue asking Jesus questions and listening to Jesus can be a model for us to engage young folk in our midst. How many of our congregations are familiar with the young adults in their midst? Are we welcoming in a way that they can come and feel free to ask us questions? Do they think we will listen to them as we expect them to listen to us? In too many of our congregations we do not have this same comfort level with young folk. The reality is their presence makes us uncomfortable.

At times, congregations deal with their discomfort by trying to find a mitigated solution. For example, we may not want to go as far as modeling the engagement in Luke 2:41-48a, but we are willing to give them special days when they can be seen and do their thing. A young adult, who we will call Sam, was a part of a congregation that had about eighty in worship. This congregation, like many, was declining and wanted more young folk to join with them. Sam was about twenty-eight and had grown up in this particular congregation. Sam had participated in all the special days and was beloved by the congregation, or so he thought. Sam wanted to become one of the rotating liturgists who participated in Sunday worship. Sam was given the runaround about needing training and how it would mean someone else would have to lose out. Sam tried to point out that he wanted to be added on and not subtract anyone and he was willing to be trained (although he was confident he could do it since he had done it on special occasions). The bottom line is they did not want Sam to participate because he was young. They were not comfortable with Sam being in such a role.

There are too many congregations like the one Sam attended that are just not comfortable with young folk being an active part of the congregation. These congregations, like Sam's, wonder why young folk are staying away. What these congregations should be asking is, why would they come? We have to construct communities where individuals feel comfortable being a part of it and not rigid communities like the one Sam belonged too. The model we find in Luke 2:41-48a is an inclusive community where Jesus felt welcomed. This is the type of community we should be seeking in our congregations.

Sampling

A few chapters later in Luke 4:18-20, Jesus comes out of the wilderness and immediately goes to the temple. Our focus at this point is not Jesus's age, but the way in which he seeks to help the people to see something new by sampling from the past. Unlike when he was a boy, those in the temple are not as excited by his presence this time. We know those in the temple are familiar with Jesus because they give him the scroll to read from Isaiah. Jesus samples from Isaiah 61 and 58. Jesus reminds those present of Isaiah's words. We talked in the beginning of this chapter about the power of sampling. Sampling is a nod to the past being incorporated into what is taking place in the present. When sampling is done well you hear the original beat, but at the same time realize something new is taking place.

Those gathered in the synagogue that day heard the words from Isaiah, words that would be familiar to them. Yet we know the people were thinking something else may be happening, because in Luke 2, verse 20, it tells us all eyes were fixed upon Jesus. The people were waiting to hear why Jesus chose these particular passages. In verse 21, Jesus tells them, "Today this Scripture has been fulfilled in your hearing." I can just imagine the excitement and joy that filled the space when Jesus tells them "today this Scripture has been filled in your hearing."

The words from Isaiah sounded reassuring to the many who were suffering. To those who hoped for freedom from Roman rule these words also sounded pleasing to the ears. If you are going to sample from the original, then Jesus picked the right words to sample. In verse 22, we learn that all were speaking well of Jesus because they are happy with what he said.

Let's put a pin in the text for just a minute! Many of our congregations are like those in the synagogue. When someone, especially someone young comes in and upholds tradition in the way that they understand, all is well. When someone young comes in and promotes their agenda, all is well. When someone young comes in and seems to be fitting in with their vision, then all is well. In fact they will probably speak highly of them.

Let's remove that pin and continue with the text. Jesus could have let the people stay right there and be happy with his words, but instead in verse 23 he starts shaking their foundation. In Luke 2, verse 24, Jesus pretty much destroys the foundation. Jesus tells the individuals that the words they have heard are true, but not necessarily true in the way they would like. Jesus reminds them in verse 23 that Elijah was only sent to a certain widow in Zarephath in Sidon and not to others in the land.

The folk in the synagogue now are upset. The words are from the prophet Isaiah, but Jesus's interpretation challenges their understanding. Jesus is claiming that this message is not for them, but for others. Wow! This had to be a hard pill to swallow. Jesus samples these great words from the prophet Isaiah and everyone is excited. Jesus undercuts all of the excitement when suggesting the words are not for them. No wonder in verse 28 the individuals in the synagogue run Jesus out of town. Literally run him out of town.

Before we agree too quickly with Jesus, as a congregation we need to look in the mirror. Like those in the synagogue, we are happy when we think someone is going to uphold the traditions or go along with "our" vision. Like those in the text, when we hear that the words are true, but not entirely for us, we often try to run the pastor or leader out of town. We cannot fathom that something new could be taking place.

For example, the idea that the congregation is called to live these words out in the community with those who are not a part of the congregation seems foreign. Many are thinking, "Certainly the message is for those of us who have been faithful all of this time." The message is for all of us who have been faithful, but not in the way we were expecting. The message is to go out and share the good news with those, who like the widow of Zarephath, are

117

not in our congregations. It means going to where the young people are and not expecting them to come to us.

A congregation seeking to do campus ministry that was next door to a college campus could not figure out why the students would not come to them. They created all kind of flyers and material but the results were minimal. Finally, they decided to try something radical: go out to the quad and engage the students. They got the appropriate permissions and started playing music in the quad. Students would stop and listen. When the band would take a break they would pray for students who were open to being prayed for by participants from the church. An amazing thing happened; they started building a ministry with the students because they went to the students and did not expect the students to come to them.

Fresh

Jesus tried to prepare those in his home synagogue for the new reality of ministry that no longer was internally focused. The new reality of ministry sampled from what was old, but expanded the reach of its message to those who were not a part of the original audience. The truth is it was not well received by those who were a part of his home synagogue. The new reality for many congregations today is not being well received. They, like those in Jesus's day, want the message to be for them and not expanded to others.

Expanding the reach of the message is exactly what we are called to do. At one level, sampling is about borrowing from what is old and repackaging it for a new audience. When someone who is twenty today hears the beats to "The Payback" in the background of several songs, it should sound a bell in his or her head that these beats are being sampled into the new hit. The question is, "Is it a good mix?" How well does the new recording integrate with the beats from "The Payback"?

A good sample maintains the integrity of both the old and the new so that the current audience experiences something fresh. By fresh I mean it is not the old song and the new production would not be the same without it. This is what Jesus does in the Luke 4 text. The integrity of Isaiah is maintained, but the new reality of expanding the message to those who are not a part of the original audience would not make sense without the Isaiah text.

The sampling Jesus does works because it maintains the integrity of the Isaiah text and the new message of reaching out to new audiences is incomplete without the Isaiah text. Jesus creates something fresh. As congregations we are called to do the same thing. We have to create something fresh and not continually repeat what we have always done. The key is that just because it is fresh does not mean it negates that which is old or traditional. The best fresh expressions include that which came before as a way of moving forward.

An individual we will call Steve wanted to do a new church plant that was focused on bringing in nonchurched young adults. Steve did all of the background work of looking at census data and what other congregations were doing trying to figure out where to plant. Steve read all the latest books on planting and on young adult trends. Steve met weekly with his team and shared all of the latest data. Because of the work Steve was doing he figured the team was ready to plant the church. They knew exactly what all the data told them and were ready to go.

Steve happened to be talking about all of his plans and how he had done all of this wonderful research with one of his friends, Kim, who did not attend church. Steve told her about his team from the mother church who would help to make the plant a success. Kim listened patiently, but finally interrupted and asked, "Have you actually talked to nonchurched young adults in the area?" Steve was startled by the question because he figured he had done all of the research needed on young adults; it never dawned on him to talk with them.

Steve learned in talking with nonchurched young adults that some of his data was good, but other parts of it were faulty. Steve was able to alter his plans because he started including those he was seeking to reach in the planning. What Kim shared with Steve was not new, but one of the foundational principles of church planting—talk to the audience you are seeking to reach. Steve learned how to take a new fresh approach to planting by pulling from church planting tradition along with doing all the new stuff he was researching. It is not old versus new, but understanding how the two can move us toward something fresh.

Thou Shall Sample

The ninth commandment is Thou Shall Sample. All congregations today need the ability to integrate that which is old or traditional with something new to create a fresh expression. The ability to reach younger individuals does not mean negating that which is old, but simply doing the same things will not work. As

I pointed out in the beginning of the chapter, negative sampling is not helpful because it does not provide us with a fresh expression to move forward. A fresh expression that moves us forward helps a new audience to see with fresh eyes the good news. This is what Joshua tries to do in the Numbers 14:6-9 text and it is what we are called to do today. We are called to be the best samplers of the tradition as we continually seek to connect with younger generations.

Covenant Practice: Inclusive Message

1. Discuss the history of your church. When was it founded? By whom? What was the original vision for the church as you understand it? How has your church's vision and mission changed over the years?

2. Has your congregation promoted positive or negative sampling of the tradition? How so? Read Numbers 14:1-3, 6-9.

3. In what ways is your congregation like those in Jesus's home synagogue not wanting to hear that the message is not just for them? How can you address these issues?

4. How are you listening to your community? How might you do this better?

5. What fresh expression may be appropriate for your congregation at this time in reaching out to a new audience?

Tenth Commandment

Thou Shall Represent: The Future Is Now!

Represent: Go and be a good example to the others of your group or in your position[1]

We previously talked about the change of leadership (chapter 6) from Numbers 1 to the list in Numbers 13 where Joshua and Caleb are included. Moses realizes that it is Joshua's and Caleb's generation that will live out the covenant with God in the promised land and that they must be included now as a part of the future. Congregations have to *represent* the future now! This chapter picks up from the last one and helps congregations to engage in innovative thinking and practices.

Jeremiah

The prophet Jeremiah grew up in a patriarchal society that privileged hierarchy, position, and age. Jeremiah was raised to wait in line and wait his turn. Do not overstep your boundaries. Be seen and not heard. So there is no surprise that Jeremiah hesitated when

123

the word of the Lord came to him saying, "Before I formed you in the womb I knew you, before you were born I set you apart; I appointed you a prophet to the nations."[2] Jeremiah tried to refuse his call. The self-described "child" (verse 6), Jeremiah was terrified to live into the call of God on his life, because he felt he was too young and ill-equipped for the journey. Whether perceived or real, many members of post-civil rights generations do not feel as if there is a place for them in today's congregations. From congregational entrenchment to leadership hierarchies to generational misunderstandings, post-civil rights generations have a lot to overcome in order to feel as if they belong in many of today's congregations. From birth, members of these generations have been told, "You are the future." Thirty-something years later, the future is now!

Not unlike in today's church, Jeremiah was programmed to wait and to bow to the will of his elders. In light of this, his only appropriate response to God was—I am not ready. Yet, God saw Jeremiah's response for what it was—an excuse. On both sides of the pew, congregations are using excuses to put off the future. On one side are the elders pointing to the post-civil rights generation: you are too young; you are not ready; you have to wait your turn and pay your dues; and you are not here enough. On the side of the post-civil rights generations, they say: you will not allow us; you will not listen to us; you do not respect us; and you do not want us here. Yet, in both circumstances, in Jeremiah's and ours, movement is required. In Jeremiah's case, God was not willing to allow Jeremiah to walk away based on Jeremiah's limited vision and understanding in the situation. When Jeremiah declared, "I'm only a child," the Lord said, "Don't say, 'I'm only a child.

Where I send you, you much go; what I tell you, you must say. Don't be afraid of them, because I'm with you to rescue you,..."[3] God goes on to describe Jeremiah's future and his call to him. God empowers Jeremiah to do the work that lies ahead and equips him for the journey. The Lord even takes the time to remind Jeremiah: "I remember your first love...how you followed me into the wilderness, in an unplanted land."[4] As a result, by the time the Lord gave Jeremiah the concrete instructions to "Go, and proclaim..." Jeremiah was ready.

Post-civil rights generations have grown weary in waiting for the arrival of the future. Everywhere else, beyond the church walls, members of post-civil rights generations are actively involved in their future. They are literally shaping the society in which we live through civic, social, economic, and technological advancement. In their jobs, they are forging new ways of working and creating new systems and thought processes, which are revolutionizing productivity and communication. Their networks have evolved beyond the imagination of generations that came before them, primarily because of their access to Internet-based communication and social networking. They cannot and will not be controlled or manipulated. Rather, they demand to be active participants in anything in which they will invest their time. Because the church has continued to call for their waiting, they are moving on in their future without the church.

Institutions and Movements

Congregations resist change. The age-old adage points out that anything that is not growing is dead. Growth and change are synonymous. One cannot happen without the other. Feet do not grow without a change in shoe size. Congregational resistance to change is a resistance to the reality that the future that it has been told to wait for, is now. In resisting change, congregations cut off growth and displace their future. A failure to recognize that the future has arrived has resulted in stagnant, aging, and dying congregations that lack generational diversity. People ask me all the time: Why is my church not growing? Why are other churches full of young people and our congregation has no children? Why do my children and grandchildren not want to come to my church? My answer: how do you and your church feel about change?

Congregations that resist change run the risk of becoming stagnate institutions. Congregations that embrace change are movements. Post-civil rights generations seek to be a part of movements rather than institutions. The Wesley brothers provide a model for congregations of today. Initially, they did not set out to start a movement, but simply to reform the Church of England. Their efforts of reformation became contagious and "The People Called Methodists" started flourishing in the 1740s. It is not until December 24, 1784, that the Methodist church officially organized in the United States. The church experienced vibrancy and growth during its early years in the United States. As the church matured and developed more institutional patterns (e.g., early days of debates over slavery, to today of dealing with complicated ordination process), it spent more energy on internal matters. Many institutions fall into this trap, spending more time on internal matters. This can cause institutions to be stale and focused on self-preservation. It is time for a new reformation effort that reclaims some of the energy, fluidity, and openness that helped to engender the original Wesleyan brothers' efforts. Our hope is this work will not be one-sided, but include all parties interested in seeing churches flourish. Movements speak to the hearts of the people. Movements are fluid and seek change for social good. Movements are open to whoever might come. Movements belong to the people and exist on behalf of the people. Movements are pliable and future-oriented.

When Representing Is Impossible

There is a single, young female who grew up in the church. She loves God and does her best to love God's people. While she openly recognizes that she does not always succeed, she sets out to live a life that is compatible with the teachings of the gospel of Jesus Christ as she understands them. When the church she grew up in split, based on a clergy-created crisis, she felt homeless. Disillusioned, she stayed away from the church for a while until she reached a point in her life that compelled her return. She spent countless Sundays and Wednesdays "trying on" new congregations. After an exhaustive search, she settled on a church where she thought she would belong and be spiritually fed. Excited about connecting with her new congregation, she attended new member classes. In the new member classes she learned about all of the ways to support her congregation's ministries. Since she has been wildly successful in her day job as a marketing executive at a large corporation, she thought she would volunteer for the communications ministry; after all, the bulletin announcement read: "all are invited and encouraged to attend."

Eager to contribute and belong, she went to the communications meeting armed with research-informed suggestions as her contribution to the meeting. When she arrived, no one welcomed her. Rather, they stared and talked among themselves about the "new" person. When the chairperson opened the meeting, she finally invited everyone to introduce themselves as they seemed to have a "visitor" to the meeting. As they proceeded through the agenda, it became clear that the communications committee was not very good at communicating in a digital age. The young woman, the only one in the room with marketing experience, made some free and cost-effective suggestions. They fell on deaf ears. She left the meeting feeling defeated and wondering if the church was really the place for her. It all started to feel too familiar to her. Having to fight at work to make herself heard until she achieved "status," she did not know whether she had the energy or will to fight at church to be heard. She never returned to the communications committee and started searching for churches again.

The church lost a committed young person with the expertise and resources to revolutionize communications in their congregation. She was again disillusioned by church people who were more concerned with position than with the future of the ministry. In their minds, she did not understand their church because she had not paid her dues and waited in line—very much the same way they did. Yet, in that same meeting, people wondered out loud about how young people hear about all of the events at the big megachurch down the street. They wondered out loud about why young people visited their church but either did not stay or did not get involved. Yet, when the "future" showed up, they were unwilling and unable to allow her to "represent." Congregations that will not make room for new people with new ideas, disallow post-civil rights generations to "represent" and to bless the congregation with the gifts that God has given them. Not allowing members of post-civil rights generations to fully participate in the life of the church hinders the opportunities for growth in them and in the congregation.

The Gospel of Innovation

Congregations that recognize that the future is now, embrace and encourage innovation. Innovation disorients and disrupts. Innovation also encourages and makes room for new people, new ideas, and new ways of being in community. God told Jeremiah "to uproot and tear down, to destroy and overthrow, to build and to plant" (Jer 1:10). These biblical directions are the definition of innovation in the church. If congregations truly recognize that the future is now, they will identify ministries, practices, traditions, ideas, and behaviors that need to be plucked up, pulled down, destroyed, and overthrown. They will sacrifice "sacred cows" in the name of progress and in order to allow for new people, ideas, ministries, practices, and traditions to be planted and built. What stands in the way of your congregation engaging in the gospel— the good news—of innovation?

Digital trepidation is one of the ways that congregations are held back from innovation. Fear of technology and its use hold congregations hostage in communicating and interacting with the people of God. Congregations that have embraced technology in worship, social media in communications, and digital availability of sermons, music, and devotional material are congregations that are engaging with new people. Congregational fights over the use of media in worship, funding for websites, and other digital disputes are signs that the congregation is resistant to innovation. *Innovation* is not a bad word. Innovation is an invitation to embrace the future orientation of the church.

When embracing innovation, congregations embrace members of post-civil rights generations. Embracing innovation sends a signal that post-civil rights generations are welcome to "represent"! Embracing innovation is a catalyst to understanding that the future is now. Signs that a congregation embraces innovation extend beyond digital engagement. A willingness to engage in different styles and curricula in Bible studies and small-group formats is a sign of innovation. Thinking beyond the church walls and traditional timing when considering locations and times to hold events is a sign of innovation. Creating spaces that are welcoming for children, youth, young adults, parents of young children, and persons who are differently abled is a sign of innovation. Exploring different styles of worship and different genres of music is a sign of innovation. Inviting nontraditional candidates to be a part of congregational leadership and decision-making bodies is a sign of innovation. To push the boundaries of what was previously understood as church is to practice and embrace innovation.

Identifying the Deal Breakers

When embracing the future as now, congregations must be clear on the deal breakers. Deal breakers are beliefs and practices that the congregation is unwilling to yield on when engaging in innovative overhauls. However, in many places, churches have identified things as deal breakers that should be up for negotiation. **Deal breakers are only to be deemed deal breakers if it is a belief or practice that risks the salvation of another.** The color of the paint on the sanctuary walls is not a deal breaker. While many hold the worship time dear, it is not a deal breaker. The meeting space of Sunday school classes is not a deal breaker. Traditions are not deal breakers. Ideas are not deal breakers. Theological practices do, however, qualify as deal breakers. The theology of a congregation, when based in scripture, tradition, reason, and experience, qualifies as a deal breaker. Almost everything else is on the list to see if it qualifies for an innovative overhaul.

Perceived deal breakers often alienate post-civil rights generations from congregations. When challenged on a practice of the congregation, most people will say, "because that's what we've always done." If we do not understand why we do what we do, and yet, are unyielding even in conversation about amending the behavior, we risk alienating new generations of potential congregants. This is not to say that congregations do not need to stand up for what they believe. Congregations must be clear and transparent about what they believe. Their actions should reinforce and serve as practical examples of their faith. Yet, congregations cannot confuse strong values and clear faith practices with long-held preferences. More times than not, perceived deal breakers are merely preferences. Real deal breakers point to the heart of faithful living.

The Terms of Engagement

Innovation usually does not happen in a linear fashion. Innovation is never clean, clear, or concise. Innovation usually does not happen on predefined or previously agreed upon terms. Innovation cannot be controlled. Innovation cannot be confined. Innovation is creative, organic, self-directed, and self-driven. Innovation requires a freedom and an authenticity in discovering a different path. Innovation requires journeying together in such a way that all involved recognize that the future is now and is unpredictable. Innovation requires trying new things in such a way that we allow for failure and success.

In serving a previous congregation, I learned to implement trial periods when trying new things. Trial periods allowed everyone involved to be heard and they fostered an atmosphere of collaborative decision-making. When introducing a new idea or a new ministry, we would be in 30-, 60-, 90-, or 100-day trial periods in which we would consistently evaluate the impact of the new idea or ministry. This allowed for multiple and dissenting voices to be heard. It provided a space in which we could say yes to new ideas from new people and the seasoned leaders did not feel left behind or ignored. By and large, new ideas that would have been given the "no" before they were able to take flight, ended up being wildly successful ministries because we gave them a chance even though we were not sure that it was worth it. Everyone, short- and long-term members, young and old congregants, rich and poor people, planners and idea people, everyone was allowed an opportunity to be heard and to shape the present future of the church.

Innovation requires doing business on new terms. Existing leadership structures may have to be reordered in such a way that they promote openness and transparency. Leadership structures need to be set up in such a way that they foster fruitful conversation and not dictatorial, adversarial decision-making. Previously unvalued opinions will need to be heard. Younger and (perceived) less experienced voices will need to be respected in the conversation. If the future is now, the future must be allowed to represent. When the future represents, the processes and the outcomes will not be the same as we are used to. Congregations that understand that the future is now redefine the terms of engagement in such a way that post-civil rights generations are free to represent as fully participating parties in the mission. If the future is now, the leadership of congregations must reflect the future. Tokenism and lip service will not do. Full participation, without perceived or real fear of retribution for disagreement, must be encouraged, pursued, and highly regarded.

A Future with Hope

Jeremiah 29 gives the church glimpses of what happens when they engage in a "the future is now" mentality. After years in exile, God speaks to the people:

> The LORD of heavenly forces, the God of Israel, proclaims to all the exiles I have carried off from Jerusalem to Babylon: Build houses and settle down; cultivate gardens and eat what they produce. Get married and have children; then help your sons find wives and your daughters find husbands in order that they too may have children. Increase in number there so that you don't dwindle away. Promote the welfare of the city where I have

sent you into exile. Pray to the LORD for it, because your future
depends on its welfare. The LORD of heavenly forces, the God
of Israel, proclaims: Don't let the prophets and diviners in your
midst mislead you. Don't pay attention to your dreams. They
are prophesying lies to you in my name. I didn't send them, declares the LORD. The LORD proclaims: When Babylon's seventy
years are up, I will come and fulfill my gracious promise to bring
you back to this place. I know the plans I have in mind for you,
declares the LORD; they are plans for peace, not disaster, to give
you a future filled with hope. When you call me and come and
pray to me, I will listen to you. When you search for me, yes,
search for me with all your heart, you will find me. I will be
present for you, declares the LORD, and I will end your captivity.
I will gather you from all the nations and places where I have
scattered you, and I will bring you home after your long exile,
declares the LORD (Jer 29:4-14 CEB).

A church that does not consider that the future is now is a
church in exile. However, it is a church that has banished itself to a
place of exile. A congregation's unwillingness to engage postmodern
generations and the future itself is a church that is exiled from its
mission. Yet, Jeremiah provides even exiled congregations a future
with hope. Jeremiah reminds exiled congregations that "dead and
dying" is not the last word. God's last word is the word of life. God's
word is to build, live, plant, eat, take, give, bear, and multiply.

Yes, it is true. Some congregations *are* too tired to build, live,
plant, eat, take, give, bear, and multiply. That is why it is so important for those congregations to invest in seeking the welfare
of their community and of the previously alienated generations.
Pray for these generations. Pray for your congregations. Pray that
God will open up avenues of conversation, relationship, and innovation so that all might move forward together. When these

congregations seek the welfare of the places and people to which they have been sent, then, and only then, will they see the promised future with hope revealed. When congregations embrace that the promised future is now, congregations will be able to seek God earnestly. When congregations seek God earnestly, then, and only then, will God bring them back from the places to which they have been exiled.

Thou Shall Represent

The tenth commandment is Thou Shall Represent. Post-civil rights generations embody the future. The future is now. The future with hope that God has promised is now. Seek the welfare of the post-civil rights generations. Seek the welfare of the communities in which you are planted. Seek God in Spirit and in truth! In seeking, you will find. In finding, you will be restored. That is the promise of God.

Covenant Practice: Innovation

1. How would you like to see your church change?

2. Read Jeremiah 1. In what ways have you or your congregation encouraged post-civil rights generations to wait their turn or disengage from your congregation's future?

3. Identify the ways in which your congregation acts like an institution. In what ways does your congregation act like a movement? Which is the predominate orientation?

4. What are the current "deal breakers" of your congregation? Which of these deal breakers should be negotiable? How will you affect that change?

5. How do you feel about innovation generally, in your personal life? Share something new you recently learned or something that has recently motivated you to do something differently.

6. Where are places that your church could engage in innovative practices? Who do you need to help you enter this season?

Conclusion

We warned you at the beginning that this book was NSFC. It seems you were willing to take the risk and read it (unless you are one of those individuals who skip to the end). What are you going to do now that you have viewed the NSFC content? Are you going to share it with others? Are you going to call a friend and tell them what you read? We suggest all of the above and committing to the covenant practices as a way forward.

The covenant practices are not meant to be steps, but practices that if your congregation commits to doing will help them to engage post-civil rights generations differently. The questions are meant to help you move forward. Here is a quick review of the covenant practices. Covenant practice one is a willingness to **let go** of the way things have been done and not stay entrenched in old ideas. Covenant practice two is a willingness to be **authentic** and stop trying to be something you are not. Covenant practice three is a challenge to be **bold** in dealing with the elephants at your own church. Covenant practice four is the need to **disrupt conventional thinking** so that your congregation will stop digging holes for itself. Covenant practice five is understanding the need for **various entry points** and not just worship. Covenant practice six is understanding that God's plan for post-civil rights leadership is **resilient** no matter how hard congregations try to prevent it from happening. Covenant practice seven is a willingness **to go** out and not expect others to come to you. Covenant practice eight is about really **listening** to those in post-civil rights generations. Covenant practice nine is a reminder that the gospel message is **inclusive** for all generations. Covenant practice ten encourages congregations to **innovate** and not simply repeat the same old thing.

These practices are not a twelve-step program, but they will help you begin to transform the culture of your congregation if you engage them seriously. This means praying for God's guidance as you engage in these practices and doing these practices over and over again until they become habitual. The questions at the end of each chapter will help you to think deeper about each practice, so make good use of the questions.

Warning: Not everyone wants to change. But you only need a few dedicated individuals to get things started. The transformation is not going to take place overnight; in fact, it is likely to take a year or two. Do not be discouraged and keep practicing! The transformation will happen!

Notes

Introduction

1. Tatted up means that a person has tattoos.

2. Brad Bryan, a student at Saint Paul School of Theology, used The Ten Commandments of Hip Hop in his final paper and we, the authors, would like to thank him for his idea.

First Commandment

1. *Urban Dictionary*, "Chill," accessed March, 7, 2013, http://www.urbandictionary.com/define.php?term=chill.

Second Commandment

1. *Urban Dictionary*, "Front," http://www.urbandictionary.com/define.php?term=front.

2. Dietrich Bonhoeffer, *The Cost of Discipleship* (London: SCM Press, 2001), Kindle edition.

3. February 1, 1963, *Time* magazine.

4. Peter J. Gomes, *The Good Life: Truths That Last in Times of Need* (New York: Harper Collins, 2002).

5. John M. Buchanan, "Editor's Desk: The young and the generous," *The Christian Century*, January 3, 2014, http://www.christiancentury.org/article/2013-12/young-and-generous.

6. Jeffrey Arnett and Elizabeth Fishel, "Generation Me? Maybe Not!," *AARP,* October 10, 2011, http://www.aarp.org/relationships /friends-family/info-10-2011/empathetic-generation.2.html.

7. Cara Newton, "Millennials: The Giving Generation?," *USA Today,* December 11, 2013, http://www.usatoday.com/story/news/na tion/2013/12/11/millennials-most-giving/3962781/.

8. Luke 12:48b CEB.

Third Commandment

1. *Urban Dictionary,* "Trippin'," accessed July 7, 2013, http://www .urbandictionary.com/define.php?term=trippin.

2. Num 13:3c CEB.

3. Num 13:17-20 CEB.

4. 2 Tim 1:7 CEB.

5. Richard Foster, *Prayer: Finding the Heart's True Home* (Grand Rapids: Zondervan, 1992), 122-124.

Fourth Commandment

1. Ice Cube, "Check Yo Self," accessed March, 13, 2013, http://www .azlyrics.com/lyrics/icecube/checkyoself.html.

2. My retelling of the story is used with permission. No names or congregational affiliations are used.

3. We realize this is not the way Ice Cube is using the phrase, but we are adapting for this context.

Fifth Commandment

1. *Urban Dictionary,* "How I Roll," http://www.urbandictionary .com/define.php?term=how+I+roll.

2. James F. White, *Introduction to Christian Worship,* 3rd ed. (Nashville, Abingdon Press, 2001), Kindle edition.

3. Justo L. González, "The Ridiculous Incongruity of Worship," *Discerning the Spirits,* Cornelius Plantinga Jr. and Sue A. Roseboom (Grand Rapids: Wm. B. Eerdmans Publishing Co., 2003), 2.

4. Edward P. Wimberly, *African American Pastoral Care* (Nashville: Abingdon Press, 1991), 26.

5. Melva Wilson Costen, *African American Christian Worship*, 2nd ed. (Nashville: Abingdon Press, 2007), Kindle edition.

6. United Methodist Church Vital Congregations Initiative, www.umvitalcongregations.org.

Sixth Commandment

1. Gadson is no longer the pastor of St. Mark's United Methodist Church in Sumter, South Carolina. She was reappointed in 2012 by the bishop.

Seventh Commandment

1. *Urban Dictionary*, "Got Game," http://www.urbandictionary.com/define.php?term=got+game.

2. Num 13:1-3 CEB.

3. Num 13:30 CEB.

4. Edwin H. Friedman, *A Failure of Nerve: Leadership in the Age of the Quick Fix* (New York: Church Publishing, Inc. 1999, 2007), 1.

5. Matt 10:6-8 CEB.

6. John 21:15-19 CEB.

7. Steve Corbett and Brian Fikkert, *When Helping Hurts: How to Alleviate Poverty Without Hurting the Poor…and Yourself* (Chicago: Moody Publishers, 2012), Kindle edition.

8. Thomas Edward Frank, *The Soul of the Congregation: An Invitation to Congregational Reflection* (Nashville: Abingdon Press, 2000), 20.

9. Peter Gomes, *The Good Life: Truths that Last in Times of Need* (New York: HarperOne, 2003), 4.

Eighth Commandment

1. *Rap.Genius*, "The Swag Song Lyrics," accessed March 25, 2013, http://rapgenius.com/1501944/Jusreign-the-swag-song/.

2. F. Douglas Powe Jr., *New Wine, New Wineskins: How African American Congregations Can Reach New Generations* (Nashville: Abingdon Press, 2012), 89.

3. David Kinnaman and Gabe Lyons, *unChristian: What a New Generation Really Thinks about Christianity…And Why It Matters* (Grand Rapids: Baker Books, 2007), 219.

Ninth Commandment

1. *Kevin Nottingham: The Underground Hip Hop Authority,* "Top 10 Most Sampled Songs in Hip Hop," blog entry by Kevin Nottingham, March 16, 2009, accessed September 10, 2013, http://www.kevinnottingham.com/2009/03/16/top-10-most-sampled-songs-in-hip-hop/.

2. Ibid.

3. *NME,* "When Sampling Goes Wrong," blog entry by Lucy Jones, September 27, 2012, accessed September 17, 2013, http://www.nme.com/blogs/nme-blogs/when-sampling-goes-wrong.

Tenth Commandment

1. *Urban Dictionary,* "Represent," http://www.urbandictionary.com/define.php?term=represent.

2. Jer 1:5.

3. Jer 1:6-8 CEB.

4. Jer 2:2 CEB.

CPSIA information can be obtained
at www.ICGtesting.com
Printed in the USA
LVOW10s0615180417
531154LV00010B/130/P